Birthing the DREAMER IN YOU

13 INSPIRATIONAL STORIES TO ACTIVATE YOUR DREAMS & RELEASE THE WEALTH WITHIN YOU!

COMPILED BY
KISHMA A. GEORGE

Birthing the Dreamer in You

Copyright © July 2021

By K.A.G. (Kishma A. George Enterprises)

Published in the United States of America by

ChosenButterflyPublishing LLC

www.cb-publishing.com

Cover design CTS Graphic Designs

Contents

Designed to Dream

By Rodney Davis

What do biblical figures like Abraham, Jacob, Joseph, Caleb, and Solomon have in common with GOD? As well as being great men of faith, they were determined dreamers. Before GOD was a provider, a healer, and a very present help in the time of trouble, He was first a dreamer. He is a relentless dreamer. His book, the Bible, is full of His dreams coming into reality. One of God's greatest dreams was to have a family of sons and daughters to share His authority and dominion with them. Thus, he created us in His image and likeness and put inside us not only the ability to procreate but His awesome nature to dream. In a sense, we are God's dream team.

1. Merriam Webster defines a dream as:

2. A series of thoughts, images, or emotions.

A strongly desired goal or purpose.

Understanding this definition, we see that God has given us His same nature to have deep longings, strong desires, and visions. We are designed to dream. And if He's given us this ability to have dreams, then there must be a way to fulfill them. Fulfilling our God-given dreams is what gives us purpose. If you are going to fulfill your dreams and visions from God, and take possession of His promises, you have to first follow Him with your whole heart. You cannot follow half-heartedly. God requires for you to be all in. The Bible informs three times in Joshua 14 that because Caleb wholeheartedly followed the Lord, the God of Israel, he was blessed with the land of his dreams called Hebron. The Bible is more than a book of rules and laws, but it is a book of dreams and power principles or cheat codes to accomplishing our dreams.

Dream It

First of all, your dreams should be so big that they give your faith a job. Your faith is unemployed until you give it something big to believe God for. If you can accomplish your dreams by yourself and without any help from Him, then it's not a dream from God. God will never give you a vision for your life that you can accomplish without Him. Not only that, but a God-sized dream is a dream that God gives you and attaches His dream to it. That is what makes your dream so big.

In Genesis 12:1–3, God gave Abram a dream. He told Abram that He would make him a great nation, bless him, make his name great, make him a blessing, bless those who blessed Abram and curse those who cursed him. As God was giving Abram this dream, God shared and connected his dream to Abram's dream. God said, "And all the people on the earth will be blessed through you." God's dream was about how He would bless the world—through Abram's dream. In that one moment, God shifted Abram's dream from personal success to significance.

God-sized dreams are not just about making your name great but making a significant difference in the lives of others. I wonder what would happen if you ever expanded your thought process concerning your personal visions and dreams to see how God's dreams are connected. Honestly, I believe you would see that God has a dream on the inside of you that has the power to bless the world. Imagine that!

Never limit yourself because of somebody else's limited imagination. Do not allow people to keep you asleep just because they haven't dreamed what you dreamed. Ultimately, the Savior of the world—Jesus—would come from Abram's God-given dream. In other words, out of Abram's dream from God came saving power. Dreams have the power to save. Jacob's beloved son—Joseph—his dream saved a nation. God's dream saved the world. Imagine how many can be saved by you fulfilling your God-given dream.

Desire It

If you are going to take your dreams to the next dimension, achieve success and great significance, you must first have a burning desire to have it. You can't just wish upon a star for it to happen. You won't be able to put on a magic cape or get bitten by a spider and all of a sudden have super powers. However, it must be a deep longing and a strong desire. Every desire is first preceded by a thought. Proverbs 23:7 says, "For as he thinks in his heart, so is he." French philosopher René Descartes said, "I think, therefore I am." In other words my thoughts produce desires within me to become all that I have envisioned. So the first step to bringing forth the dream is to have a burning desire for it. Mix that desire with the belief that you will become it. Your belief must be so strong that you are willing to burn all other bridges for it and have no plan B.

One Saturday, I was attending a prophetic prayer breakfast, and the keynote speaker, who is a powerful woman of God, called me out. She proceeded to tell one of her helpers to bring me some eggs and a basket. They gave me the eggs and put the basket next to me. As she kept on delivering a powerful word, she would periodically glance at me to ask if I got it yet. A few times I said no because I didn't have a clue why this woman would have me holding some eggs all through the service. Then it hit me. God opened up the eyes of my understanding to realize that she wanted me to put the eggs into the basket. You are probably thinking, *It didn't take a rocket scientist to figure that out.* Nevertheless, the woman of God wanted me to understand that unless I am willing to cut all other ties and put all of my hopes and dreams into one basket, I will not possess the promise. I was in awe because at the time I was playing it safe and was dipping and dabbing in various opportunities. At that moment, I realized that believing is not just trusting God not knowing how He is going to work it out, but it's trusting God to the point that you put all of your eggs into one basket. There is no backup plan. There is no plan B. You are all in.

Not too long ago, I heard a story about a ruler that wanted to conquer and possess a new land he had spied out, so he and all of his soldiers traveled by ships to this new land. When they arrived, he ordered some men to burn all of the ships. He said to his army, "Either we conquer this land or we die." Needless to say, they ended up conquering the land. The point is desire must be at the forefront of every God-given dream, and it must be mixed with the belief that what you are longing for is the purpose of God for your life. According to Psalm 27:4, King David said, "One thing have I desired of the Lord, that will I seek after…" Notice, David did not chase after a bunch of dreams. He only went after one.

What is the one burning desire that you've been dreaming about? The one goal that, if you were to achieve it, would transform your life. The one vision that, if you pursued it, so many souls would benefit from it. Stop hitting the snooze button on your desires because God communicates with you through them. Not only does God speak through angels, dreams, the Holy Spirit, promptings, and His Word, but He also speaks to us through desires. Psalm 37:4 says, "Delight yourself in the Lord and he will give you the desires of your heart." When you delight in God, through your desires is how He communicates back to you. Secondly, desires will also cause you to develop action plans and that is when creativity will begin.

Let's take a look at God's example of this. God had a dream, developed an action plan or vision, and then began creating. In other words, creativity doesn't happen without first having a dream. In Jeremiah 1:5, God says, "Before I formed you in the womb I knew you, before you were born I set you apart." The word knew is the Hebrew word "yada," which means to intimately see; to perceive and be well acquainted with. God was saying that not only did He have a reoccurring dream about Jeremiah, but He also developed a game plan for his life before He created him. Psalm 139:16 says, "Your eyes saw my unformed body; all the days ordained for me were written in your book before one of them came to be." This text is suggesting God had a dream of us, wrote the vision for our lives, and then started the creation process. Hence, creativity does not happen without first having a dream. If you can dream it, God will give you the power to plan and create it.

Dreams Deferred

How you handle a temporary setback determines how successful you will be in transferring your dreams from thought into reality. In Genesis 1:1–2, the Bible states, "In the beginning God created the heaven and the earth. And the earth was without form, and void; and darkness was upon the face of the deep..." Biblical scholars who lean towards the Gap Theory believe God created the world perfectly in verse one. Verse two, on the other hand, they assume that a great catastrophic event occurred that caused the earth to become chaotic, dark, and disorderly. After this the story picks up with the Spirit of God moving to restore and recreate the brokenness. Many of these theorists believe the chaos came from Satan's rebellion and fall. And that fall ruined God's dream for the earth, making it desolate and uninhabitable. If that wasn't enough, after God created man and woman, His crowning masterpiece, after He gave them authority to be fruitful, multiply, replenish, subdue, and have dominion, and after God gave them the terms and conditions, Satan came in and influenced Adam and Eve to follow a different agenda. Adam and Eve took their eyes off of the dream and sinned in the Garden of Eden. God's dream of a family was temporarily broken.

Satan loves to attack God's dream. I am certain that if Satan had the audacity to come after God's dream, he has and will send giants to come after your dreams too. Many of you reading this chapter right now feel like you've had your dreams shattered by the cataclysmic events of the past year. I encourage you to keep dreaming and keep reading this chapter. You will find new hope to pursue those broken dreams.

A little more than a year ago, the world anxiously awakened to a day that will go down in history. The coronavirus Covid-19 pandemic became the greatest challenge the world has faced since World War II. It was a global health crisis. You read about it on the front page of every newspaper. Heard about it on every news outlet. While Fox News praised the president for his response to the pandemic, CNN, MSNBC, and other media outlets criticized and questioned the president's response, strategies, and decisions. Stocks began to crash. Government offices and public schools closed their doors. Events around the world were canceled. Shortages and delays intensified. Jobs were lost. Unemployment skyrocketed. I never thought I would see the day church doors would close while liquor stores and marijuana dispensaries remained open. Almost three million people have died due to the coronavirus. And in the famous poetic words of Paul Lawrence Dunbar, "We wear the masks."

As if this global war wasn't enough, social injustice was at an all-time high. Racism gained new life. On May 25, 2020, a police officer—whose job is to protect and serve—kneeled on the neck of George Floyd, an unarmed black man, for eight minutes and 46 seconds. The world witnessed a modern-day lynching.

Floyd's death shed light on 26-year-old African American woman Breonna Taylor's tragic death. She too was shot down and killed in her apartment on March 13, 2020 by white plainclothes police officers. To the day of this writing, justice has not been given to Breonna Taylor's family. Yes, we've had some dark days we've never seen before, and dreams seemingly have been stolen in this season of life. Nevertheless, I admonish you not to give up but to dream again.

Do you know that we serve a God that knows what it is like to have broken dreams? Yet, God, in his all-knowing wisdom, had a plan to resurrect His dreams before the problem existed. That's why Revelation 13:8 refers to Jesus as, "the Lamb who was slain from the creation of the world." That is to say, God had an answer before the problem existed. And the good news is He has a plan to revive your dead dreams as well. The Dream-giver's dream book has taught me that whenever God is about to do a new thing, it is often preceded by darkness. To put it another way, darkness is an indication that God is up to something. For example, after the earth became formless and void, and darkness was upon the face of the deep, the Bible says that the Spirit of God began to move and recreate. Darkness proceeded the move of the Spirit. Likewise, when Jesus was dying on the cross, the Bible let us know that at the sixth hour, or around noon, darkness fell over all the world. Jesus soon died, was buried, and raised from the dead. Whenever God is doing something new, it is often preceded by darkness. If your dreams have been shattered by this past year of darkness, know that through that darkness God has designed a greater dream for you. He knows how to rob darkness of its power to destroy.

In his book *Dream*, Dutch Sheets tells a story about a beautiful and priceless mosaic at the Royal Palace of Tehran. The architect of the mosaic originally was trying to decorate the palace walls with huge sheets of mirrors. However, as the shipments arrived, the contractor discovered that the mirrors were all shattered and broken into pieces. In frustration, the contractor threw them in the trash and proceeded to tell the architect what had happened to the mirrors. In a stroke of genius, the architect summoned the contractor to fetch all of the broken pieces of glass. The architect then took the broken pieces and smashed them into tiny pieces and glued them to the walls of the palace. In utter amazement, out of the brokenness of the glass, the architect turned a mess into a magnificent mosaic.

God is the great architect of our hopes and dreams. Jeremiah 29:11 tells us He knows the plans that He has for us. Plans to give us a hope and a future. He sees beyond our brokenness to what we can become. We must learn to put our hopes in his hand. God delights in bringing forth beauty in brokenness and creating mosaics out of messiness. If you are broken right now, keep dreaming. Pray and ask God to turn your mess into a mosaic.

I love how Job 14:7,9 states, "Even a tree has more hope! If it is cut down, it will sprout again and grow new branches... yet at the scent of water it will bud and put out branches like a young plant." When you feel like your dreams are broken and cut down, sometimes all you need to do is get around somebody who smells like a dreamer and watch your dreams flourish again. Do like Mary and Elizabeth and get around somebody who is pregnant and watch the baby God has given you leap and live again.

9

Decide It

- The number one reason many people fail to pursue their God-given dreams is because they allow procrastination to set in by their inability to make a decision and move out on it. As you go after your dreams this year, I want you to affirm these words:

- "I will decide quickly and change my mind about it slowly."

"I will only share my vision with others by the prompting of the Holy Spirit."

One of the reasons James warns us to be quick to listen and slow to speak is because he knows that there are some people who are anointed in talking us out of every word God has spoken over our lives. They will form committees just to tell you how it can't be done and that it is not your season. Giving ear to these negative voices can sometimes cause you to hesitate just long enough to miss your door of opportunity. We must understand that God is a moving God. When the world was full of darkness, the Spirit of God quickly made a decision to move and do something about it. Throughout the Old Covenant, the cloud by day and the fire by night led the people of God. In the New Covenant, we see Jesus moving immediately and straightway. Paul backs it up by saying, "For all who are led by the spirit of God are the children of God." In the last chapter of Revelation, Jesus said, "Surely I come quickly..." To put it plainly, God is a moving God and doesn't wait too long for anyone. As a matter of fact, you can find yourself backsliding from Him and falling short of His glory simply by procrastinating. Backsliding not because you went back into a sin you were delivered from but solely because you stood still while God moved on. When God gives you a dream, you must move, which means to decide quickly and take immediate action to make it happen. I believe that when you move out in pursuit of your dreams with new passion this season, God is going to manifest your dreams in front of everyone who said it wasn't your season.

Declare It

One of the greatest tools God has given us in our pursuit of dreams is the power to decree and declare. Elijah prayed both that it might rain and then that it might not. And both came to pass. In other words, he had the power to speak a season in and out of his life. Likewise, you have the power to speak certain opportunities in and out of your life. Someone once said, "God has given you the power to speak a funeral or a future." I am talking about faith. In Romans 10:17, Paul says, "So then faith comes by hearing, and hearing by the word of God." Strictly speaking, you have to repeatedly speak the Word of God or make affirmations over dreams daily. You must declare them to the degree that you believe you already have what you're declaring. That it is already done in the Spirit. The truth is it already is. Ephesians 1:3 confirms that we are "...blessed with all spiritual blessings in heavenly places." This is why Jesus said, "When you pray, believe that you have received it, and it will be yours." When you make those daily affirmations of faith over your life, your mind will begin to act on those thoughts you want it to and work hard to bring it to pass. To be clear, if your affirmations are not backed by faith in

11

God, no matter what you say, they will not work for you. I believe this is why God says in Isaiah 29:13, "These people worship me with their mouths, and honor me with their lips, but their hearts are far from me. And they worship me in vain." Simply put, lip service doesn't work without faith.

In your effort to pursue your God-given dream, you must dream it, desire it, decide on it quickly, and declare it and, lastly, discern it.

Discern It

To discern means to see; to perceive by sight or some other sense or by intellect; to apprehend. Simply put, discern means to have vision. Myles Munroe said, "Eyes that look are common, but eyes that can see are rare." Vision forms action plans to what you are dreaming. Habakkuk 2:1 said, "I will stand at my guard post and station myself on the ramparts. I will watch to see what He will say to me, and how I should answer when corrected." What is interesting in this text is that the prophet said he will "watch" to "see" what God will say. The one problem we glean from the text is that usually when we are waiting for someone to say something we don't usually use our eyes to see what they are saying. For most of us, we typically use our ears to hear what a person is saying. I believe there is a hidden truth behind this saying. That truth is that whenever God is speaking to us, we must translate what He said into something we can visualize and get a clear picture. I believe that's why Habakkuk continues in the second verse and says, "Write the vision." Notice, he didn't say the Lord said, "Write what you heard me say," but, "Write what you saw when I was speaking. Write down what you imagined." If you are going to go after your God-given dreams you must be visionary. A visionary sees beyond finance and success to significance. Visionaries see past what is to what it could be. Jesus didn't just see fishermen, he saw disciples. He didn't see a prostitute but a preacher and follower in Mary of Magdala. Christ didn't just see sinners, but he saw a bride in us. Make sure to write that vision down as plainly as possible. Include everything you imagined when God shared it with you even if it seems unbelievable to you and others. This is not the hour to limit yourself because of somebody else's limited imagination. To say it another way, do not allow people to keep you asleep just because they haven't dreamed what you dreamt. You are the only person who has a balcony view to your vision. Everyone else only has a basement view.

Proverbs 29 first 18 states, "Where there is no vision the people perish." Notice it didn't say where there is no husband or wife, house or car, family or church. The word said where there is no vision. In other words, either you are going to dream or you are going to die. Maybe not a physical death but certainly a figurative death. The word for perish is the Hebrew word "para," which means without restraint. Where there is no vision, people are without restraint. When you look at trees growing without restraint in the forest, you discover that every day of the lives of those trees they are in competition. They are constantly trying to out-position the other trees in the pursuit of getting more of the sunlight they need to grow and tower over the other trees. In the same way, people without a vision will always be in competition against others and politicking for positions and titles.

This word "perish" also means uncontrolled, like a car without brakes. Where there is no vision, people are out of control and headed for self-destruction. They are unbridled, which means they run wild and rogue. However, those with vision are in control, headed for success, self-disciplined, and know who they are. A person with vision won't get distracted. He won't waste a lot of time working in a field that is not a part of his vision. She won't waste all of her time in a relationship with a man who cannot cover her. A person with vision is a joyful person to be around.

I declare that as you apply these power principles to your dreams, God will release a greater level of visions and dreams upon you. I declare God is sending you multiplied vision. You are about to dream in an outrageous way. Think it not strange that your dreams will disturb some family members in this season. God is causing your dreams to make you remarkable. You've been invisible long enough and now God is about to make you stand out. You are going to be the next living testimony. I declare that your dreams are about to heal you in every area you've been hurting and lacking. Ultimately, I declare and decree that God will use your dreams to fulfill His dreams to bless a generation of people. In Jesus' name. Amen.

Rodney's Acknowledgements.....

I wish to give all glory to God for the thirst He has placed in me, and the desire He has given me to follow after Him. I further thank God every day for the extraordinary support and joy He has placed in my life, without which I could do so much less.

My wife, my perfect gift from God, backs me up, holds me up, and pushes me forward. She is always there, ready to serve and answer any call. I am respected in my home and at the city gates due in part to my virtuous wife.

My children and grandson: La Shelle, Jenna, Adonijah, Leah, Eden, Micah, and Joshua are an unending source of joy and pride! They amaze me every day with their differences, strengths, and determination.

I thank my parents-Shirley and Lonzo, my extended family, especially my aunts and uncles, and my Transformation Church family for their vigilant support in abiding with me on this journey.

Meet author Rodney Davis

LEADER

Elder Rodney Davis, husband and father of six, is the pastor of Transformation Church, where his purpose is to pattern the heartbeat of God's people after the heartbeat of God by presenting a Christian paradigm, equipping and motivating men and women who desire to fulfill God's purpose for their lives through the arts, ministry, and education, and providing the practical and spiritual groundwork needed to achieve success and significance.

EDUCATOR

Rodney Davis received his Bachelor of Arts degree from Delaware State University, majoring in English and Music Education. For over 15 years he has worked with students enrolled in adult education programs and alternative schools and is currently working as a kindergarten teacher in the 90 | Designed to Dream Capital School District. In 2011, he was named Educator of the Year by the Omega Psi Phi Fraternity, Inc.

You can connect with Rodney via

Web: www.transformationofde.com

Email: Transformationchurchde@yahoo.com

Facebook: @rodney.davis3

Instagram: @pastorrldavis

Twitter: @Roddav

It's your Time

By Nicole Bryant

Have you ever stopped to think about Yourself? Yes, that's right ... You! Have you considered all of the things you want out of life? Personally speaking, it took a long time for me to stop and think about myself and what I wanted in life. While I had questioned for the longest, "What is my true purpose?" I concluded and decided that "It's My Time!" After living my life taking care of everybody else and ensuring that they were okay, when I reflected on my life, I realized that none of the things I wanted out of life at that time were being fulfilled. When it was all said and done, I stopped one day and thought, What about me? Let me take you on my life's journey.

When I was a child, I had stepped in as the 'mother' when my mother went to work. Before I knew it, I became the 'mother', teacher, mentor, and cook. Even though the tasks required a lot of work, I found that it was still okay because it never felt like a job. I understood that things had to be taken care of and the fact of the matter was that someone had to do it. I was also the go-to person for my friends. They felt comfortable always coming to me for guidance and advice. I was always there making sure they were good after bad relationships, deaths, and health issues.

Again, at times it felt difficult, but I figured, "That's what friends are for," and I still served and helped others. Moving on in life and having a family of my own, I not only became the wife but the enemy as well. This was because I would not "bow down to bail" (meaning doing things that were not conducive for our home). You can't care about things properly when everything becomes optical. At some point, it doesn't even matter anymore to you. When that happens, you give up the fight and save your energy for someone who wants it. Love comes in all forms and fashions, and you always rise to the occasion for the ones you love.

Despite the condition of my marriage, I had a love so great for my mother-in-law that I became her caregiver up until her transfer to a hospice. I knew that my time and energy were needed by someone who wanted it and appreciated it. My mother-in-law passed, and, not too long after, the marriage died as well. While I didn't know it at the time, some many years later, I would be flying back and forth to take care of my mother. She refused to relocate for care, and even though the journey was long that didn't faze me because it was my mother, and I would run through fire for her if I had to. When her journey ended in 2010, my mother took her last breath with me holding her hand.

I was now left with so many questions: What do I do? Who do I take care of? What problem do I try to fix? Who should I cook meals for? There were so many questions, but I had no answers at all. The Bible asks us a question in 1 Corinthians 11:28 KJV, "Will a man examine Himself?" and that was the point in my life when I arrived at self-examination. It was through looking in the mirror that I came to realize, "It's Your Time! YES, it's time to live for you. It is time to achieve your dreams and visions. Think! What has happened to your dreams and visions? Did you simply bury them with everything else?" I had once written all of my dreams on a piece of paper. I wrote it all down and opted to put it in a safe place so long ago, but some time had passed and I realized that it was still sitting on that piece of paper. "What about your desires and goals?" Well, at that moment a fire sparked in me and I realized that it was my time to live the life that I was still expecting to live. Oh, and did that fire burn. I felt like Jeremiah with fire shut up in my bones (Jeremiah 20:9 KJV). I felt life restoring to me as if I had died as well but now I was Resurrecting.

I have always felt the need to help others. My passion for helping goes back a long way; besides my family and friends, I volunteered as a mentor for elementary school children at P.S. 399 while in Walt Whitman Junior High School. In high school, I also volunteered at Calvary Cancer Hospital. Later, I would work at Long Island College Hospital and would pursue college twice for nursing. However, I would never finish after arriving at the realization that my heart was too sensitive to deal with the daily grief that came with the job. At this point in life, I began to ask, "What do I do? How do I continue to help those in need and offer what I have to give?" After meeting those questions head-on, I began to work in a hair salon.

Working in a hair/beauty salon allows you to help transform those who don't feel beautiful due to life circumstances; to help them see their true beauty. I find that we live in a harsh and cruel world, but the joy you see when an individual's smile and attitude change after getting their hair or nails done helps you to know you made a difference once again. God will place you in the right place at the right time when you least expect it.

After some significant career changes, I had to seek employment and started work at a beauty school. Working at the beauty school brings me such joy because I can see the difference I can make every day in the lives of those God chooses to cross my path according to His will. It is life-changing when you can inspire and encourage some women who have never had any real form of guidance and support. It is equally rewarding to see some students with low self-esteem transform in less than 12 months due to the strength of your ability to facilitate a change. As a teacher, I developed a profound concern for those students who seemed like they have only dealt with lemons in life. Metaphorically speaking, I felt that it was my duty to show them how to make lemonade. When you come to a point where you realize that your personal experiences are stepping stones to help others, you can show others how to get through and hold their head up. Instances like this encourage you to continue to push, not necessarily just for yourself but for others as well.

After spending time knowing that you were created for a purpose but never really knowing what it was, finally figuring it out gives you strength. Once you find out that you are a Purpose-Pusher, a Spiritual-Midwife, a Chain breaker, and a Yoke-destroyer, you put on your War clothes and get ready for the battle (for others and yourself). Despite this, after some years of always battling for myself and others, I realized that this still wasn't enough. There was more on the inside of me, and it was always bubbling up to be released. So, I spent more time with myself and would ask, "How can we let others realize they're not alone? More specifically, how do we get females to see this?" These questions sparked my interest in holding a conference. The name of my conference was "P.U.S.H. - Push past the pain to pursue Purpose." So many times, we get stuck in all the downfalls, setbacks, heartbreaks that we forget that when God created us, He created us for our Purpose. It is good to help others, but I've discovered that we cannot help others if we don't first help ourselves.

The conference was life-changing: it served as a platform for women to give their testimonies on topics ranging from health to ministry and everything in between. I made it a "safe place" with no access to social media or recording of any type ensuring safety for both the speakers and guests. In a short span after the conference, a pandemic came to the land. Our world went into a complete shutdown due to the COVID-19 virus. We all began to experience life as we had never seen it before. Some of the women would call me after the conference and extend their thanks. They would call and say, "I thank you because I needed that." Some of the young girls remarked that they wanted to make better decisions so they wouldn't have to go through the same obstacles they had before. I felt inspired and more passionate to help after seeing the difference that the conference made. I felt very accomplished that I had such a massive impact despite a pandemic and the worldwide shutdown. I started a nonprofit organization and was led to name it P.U.S.H.-Pushing Until Shifting Her LLC. My vision was: Let's push young girls and women until they shift. She may not feel like moving or may be moving at a slower capacity than she should, but I am my sister's keeper; therefore, I won't allow her to stay in that stuck place. The conference birthed a nonprofit that would help any female realize and fulfill her Purpose in life. No matter the reason for a female being and feeling stuck, we will not allow her to stay there.

After realizing my Purpose, I am now helping others fulfill theirs. The way I see it is: we all have different calls and gifts in life, but the important thing is to keep pushing and don't give up. No matter what comes our way, we cannot just throw in the towel. If we do not give up, then we can achieve anything. By not quitting, we make sure that each of our efforts is effective. I know now that "It's My Time!" to be who God created me to be and pursue the Purpose He has for me. Jeremiah 29:11 (KJV) confirms this: "For I know the thoughts that I think toward you, saith the Lord, thoughts of peace, and not of evil, to give you an expected end."

And because I believe in the God that created me, I also believe in the plans He has for me without knowing them firsthand. That's what you call Faith.

Nicole's Acknowledgements:

This is chapter is dedicated to my mother, who is no longer here but taught me never to give in and to always finish what I started, and to all the women who could not see their way through life but realize Now is Their Time to Push Forward.

Meet author Nicole Lindsay Bryant

I am a teacher, mentor, motivational speaker, business owner, certified Christian counselor, prophet, and intercessor. By profession, I am double-licensed, both as a New York State cosmetologist and as a New York State cosmetology instructor. I find that my job is where the Lord leads me to minister and transform women back to wholeness daily. I am a two-time author, with one of my works listed on the Amazon bestsellers list in three different categories. Also, I have been featured in numerous publications and magazines, such as *KISH* magazine. I have guest-starred on Christian television. Also, I have shared the Word of God in various churches and conferences to date. Currently, I am involved with numerous intercessory teams in which I pray and speak the Word of God in the United States, Caribbean Islands, and various countries weekly. After experiencing trials and setbacks from childhood to adulthood (after a divorce and the death of my mother and some of my immediate family members), I was prompted to shift myself and pursue my purpose. I began giving back even more to young girls and women by helping them find their purpose. Mentoring has always been my passion since I was a junior high schooler mentoring elementary school children once a week. On March 8, 2020, I carried out my first women's empowerment conference called P.U.S.H. (Pushing Until Shifting Her)—"Push past the hurt to Pursue Purpose." It proved to be a huge success with 150 women registered in less than two days. After that, I decided to take P.U.S.H. to the next level and became the founder and CEO of P.U.S.H. Pushing Until Shifting Her LLC. in August 2020. The mission of P.U.S.H. is to help young girls to adult women push past their hurt, pain, and setbacks to pursue their purpose. I didn't stop there; I became a certified Christian counselor in September 2020 amid a pandemic. I am truly thankful to God that He chose to use me in this season. I know it may look like I haven't been there, but it's all for my making as I continue to push.

As an overcomer of cancer, and losing my mother and numerous family members to cancer, God placed in my Spirit to have an online "Overcomer" cancer awareness conference. The conference, which took place in October of 2020, shined a light on people who had cancer, those who had lost their lives, and the caregivers affected by their loved ones. This conference was a great success, receiving 1000 views and many testimonies.

Romans 8:28 says, «And we know that all things work together for good to them that love God, to them who are the called according to His purpose,» and I thank God that He has called me.

Contact Info:

Email: Prophetess727@gmail.com

FB & IG: Nicole NHW

Radio: https://envisionedbroadcasting.com/its-your-time-pushing

God Favored Me

By Shirlene Jones

I would like to share a little of my personal journey/ testimony of how "GOD favored me!" My intent in sharing some of my story is to encourage everyone that no matter what your life has been like, it changes today. "Speak Life over your Life!" Sometimes we can write, talk out loud to ourselves, or maybe just sing a song of encouragement. From a little girl, one of my favorite songs was "The Blood." It is just something about singing and mentioning the name of JESUS that always lifts heavy burdens.

Throughout my childhood it seemed like the LORD was important to a lot of people who were connected to me, including my mom. I remember numerous times as a girl putting a few dollars in an envelope with a letter of prayer request and sending it to (Reverend Frederick J. Eikerenkoetter II) Rev. Ike or Pastor R.W. Schambach. I recall Rev. Ike would say, "You can't lose with the stuff that I use; dream your dreams." I can truly testify that we cannot lose with "The WORD of GOD" and that is what Rev. Ike and Pastor Schambach were preaching, "JESUS!" II Samuel 13:19: And Samuel grew, and the LORD was with him, and did let none of his words fall to the ground.

29

At this point, I have come to realize that every phase of life's challenges will be present, but the situations we encounter are meant to bring us closer to the FATHER. Repeatedly, I have experienced GOD'S love and power lifting me. There have been times when I felt so alone because shame was wearing me down. This is the first time that I have shared the details about my stay/testimony in North Carolina with my family or anyone. I know without a shadow of a doubt "GOD favored me!"

Initially, I believe pride kept me from sharing this chapter of my life and then after a while I blocked it. I know that I could have been raped or killed or both and no one would have known where to look for me. But GOD had a purpose for my life and HIS favor always rested upon me and others recognized there was something.

As I was growing up, I can remember hearing my mom praying. As a little girl, I heard her talking out loud; I would say, "Mommy, who are you talking to?"

She would reply, "Baby, I'm talking to LORD!"

Well, all my life I have been talking to the LORD because of the precedence that HE was given in my home as a child.

At 17, I was a virgin and very naïve to the world, so I got involved with a mean grown-up man (boyfriend). In the beginning appearances can be very deceiving; he presented as a knight in shining armor to me, especially because he always had money and he was willing to spend some of it on me. Oh, he baited and baited me until he had me where he wanted me; I loved, trusted, and relied solely on him for my truth. One day, I was commenting on how nice this other guy's car looked and my boyfriend almost slapped the taste clear out of my mouth along with the food that I was eating. That was my valley of decision, but I chose to accept his behavior because he quickly apologized and patted me up. This grown-up man became my everything and he also had other women besides me, because mind you I am still in high school.

He took me to Washington D.C. and a lot of different places that this country girl had not seen. Fast forward to 20 years old, this same grown-up man asked me to marry him. And of course, my answer was, "Yes." Proverbs 29:18 KJV: Where there is no vision, the people perish: but he that keepeth the law, happy is he.

I was so determined to marry this man, who was almost 10 years my senior. We went to the justice of the peace and were accompanied by my mom, my brother, and my stepfather. Before the ceremony started my mom asked me, "Shirl, are you sure you know what you are doing?"

I responded, "Yes, Mom, I really want to get married."

My mom was praying profusely the whole time we were exchanging our vows. In her spirit man, she knew that chaos and confusion awaited her firstborn. She started pleading the Blood of JESUS, so loud that the justice asked if everything was okay.

After we were married, the first place we stopped to was a liquor store and purchased a half gallon of Jack Daniels and some Coca-Colas. We went to visit his family to celebrate. My mother-in-law did not offer congratulations, she said, "Shirlene, you are too good for my son."

I said, "Thank you," because I knew that she really did mean well.

My husband was committing adultery for money within a month of us getting married. He contracted an STD and we had to go to the public clinic to get some pills. I was so angry; he continued to apologize. Once, I mentioned it and he started beating me up and dared me to ever bring it up again. He said, "How many_____ times am I supposed to say I am sorry?" I just kept quiet. I married a very angry and mean man; his life had made him bitter with everyone around him, but he was very good at putting on a façade for personal gain.

My mom had worked in a poultry processing plant and she did not want her children to work in one. However, after we got married, I went right to work in a "chicken factory." Imagine that; I could have gone to airline school, but no, I chose to get married and to work in a chicken factory.

We worked and I saved most of our money. By the fourth paycheck, my husband said, "We need a car." He was very inpatient, and he wanted what he wanted when he wanted it. So, we purchased a car, using our neighbor's insurance to move the car from the dealership's lot.

One icy, snowy day, we were preparing to go to work. We went outside to get into the car; my husband opened the door for me, then he walked to the driver's side. And oh my! He slipped down in the snow and I had no idea that he had a butcher's knife in his torn coat pocket. The knife was lodged in his back. He cried out, "Shirl, come take this knife out of my back."

I was terrified and cried out, "Somebody help me, please; my husband slipped and he has a knife in his back, please call 911!" I pulled the knife out of his back, kneeled beside him, prayed and trusted GOD for his life. Proverbs 3:5 KJV: Trust in the LORD with all thine heart; and lean not unto thine own understanding.

When the paramedics and the police arrived, they asked, "What happened here?" I told them, "We were about to leave for work; he let me in the car, and then all I heard was him yelling for my help." I gave the police the knife.

My husband told them, "That's the way it happened, everything my wife said is true." WOW GOD! From time to time I used to think, *What if he had lost consciousness or died before he had confirmed what I said? Who would have believed such an outlandish story?* All I can say is thank GOD for a praying Mother and GOD favored me! Jeremiah 29:11 NLT: "For I know the plans I have for you," says the LORD. "They are plans for good and not for disaster, to give you a future and a hope."

His hospital stay was about 21 days. The treating doctor told us, "Taking the knife out was the wrong thing to do."

But my husband always said, "Shirl, thank you, if you had not removed that knife I would have died."

The hospital bill was very expensive. I applied for a certain type of funding (a trust that had been established by one of the hospital benefactors for people with no medical coverage and/or hospitalization). His bill was paid in full. We were only responsible for the paramedics/transporting and a small doctor's fee.

After my husband was discharged from the hospital, he stayed around long enough to recover. And one day, when I was at work, he walked away. A few days later, he called and stated, "I am in D.C., you know I can't stay down there in the country for too long. I will be back for you in three or four months, I have to make some money." I worked and saved my money too.

One day, my husband just popped up! He said, "I am going to take you back to D.C. with me."

My Mom said, "What?"

He stated, "Shirl is my wife and I will take very good care of her, don't worry."

I hugged my Mom and said, "Don't worry, Mom, I will be fine."

We did not have a car, so we had to take the Trailway bus to Washington D.C. However, as soon as we arrived in D.C., he said, "I really want to go to Raleigh, North Carolina."

I asked, "But what about my suitcase?"

He said, "Oh, don't worry; I will buy you some new clothes." And off we went. I could feel my Mom praying for me.

I am encouraging somebody to wait on GOD for your spouse; no matter what your age is GOD has a special wife/husband just for you! Wait on GOD. Psalm 27:14: Wait on the LORD, be of good courage, and HE shall strengthen thine heart: wait I say on the LORD. GOD will never allow us to enter a situation without showing us the danger signs; however, it is our choice in which direction we choose to go.

After we arrived in Raileigh, N.C., we rented a room for several days. One day, my husband came back with two other guys and he said, "I found us a job." I asked the guys if we could speak alone and they stepped out. My husband said, "I am going to be doing a little field work and you are going to be cooking, sound okay?"

I said, "Sure."

We rode and rode until we finally arrived in Dunn, N.C. at a migrant camp (for person(s) who move from one place to another to work). We went to meet the man who oversaw the camp, his name was Jimmy. When he greeted us, my husband made the introductions for both us. Jimmy stated, "I never had a real husband and wife team working for me before; welcome and we will do our best to help you folks as much as we can."

I said, "Thank you and yes sir."

He said, "No sir, just Jimmy; that's my name."

Jimmy told the men to take us to Smithfield, N.C. because we would need some different type of clothes to go to work in the fields. It had shifted just that quickly from my husband working in the field to both of us working in the field. We went to a thrift store and picked up a few things.

While visiting North Carolina technically I was homeless, but I worked hard and paid to keep a roof over my head. We were migrant workers and stayed on what some people refer to as a "Tramp Camp."

That evening, we were given dinner, then we were given breakfast the next morning. They explained that rice was served with every meal. It was a little difficult falling asleep because we were in a totally unfamiliar place, but I slept okay. We were given sandwiches for our lunch and told the farmers would give out different types of snacks.

Our first two days, we picked cucumbers and neither one of us was very good at that, mostly because the field was so picked over. Oh my, was that hard work, did I mention hot and dirty? We got paid on Saturday, so we did a little shopping and ate dinner at the local Tastee Freeze. We rested well over the weekend to prepare for the tobacco field.

The first two days weren't bad, just long. We were breaking the sickles off the tobacco plants so they could grow bigger/taller. The next week, we started cropping the tobacco, meaning you must start at the very bottom breaking the tobacco leaves off the plants. The rows in the field where we were working seemed to be a mile long. We went down row after row after row! Wow! By the end of the week, we were exhausted. We got paid on Saturday, did our shopping, had dinner at the Tastee Freeze and rested. I listened to a church service on Sunday and my husband got up and went out. I made fried chicken, canned greens, sweet potatoes, and fried bread for dinner; it took most of the afternoon because I had to cook on a hotplate with two burners.

We worked and I saved our money. By middle of the fourth week, my husband decided that we would take a day off to relax and enjoy each other. Well, he did it again! While I was still relaxing and sleeping, he took our savings and just walked away.

When I finally woke up, I thought, *Where is he?* So, I got myself together and I came out of our room; everyone was still at work. I went over to Jimmy's trailer and asked if he had seen my husband. Jimmy said, "Several hours ago, I saw him walking down the lane." I had that sinking type feeling because our money was gone too. I mentioned that to Jimmy. I went back to my room, cried, and cried, and I quoted Psalm 23 out loud to comfort myself.

By the evening my husband still had not returned, so Jimmy called everyone including me to come out in the front yard. He said, "This little lady believes that her husband has left her here alone; well, she said she is going to stay and work. No one on this camp better not say one word out of the way to her, do we have that understanding?" He continued, "If she has any problem, I will deal with that _____ _____ myself!" I felt so embarrassed and ashamed, but I had made my mind up that I could not return home with nothing.

I want to encourage someone right now to "stop operating in the spirit of pride." I had a family who loved and cared for me. Why not go home? Proverbs 16:9 KJV: A man's heart deviseth his way: but the LORD directeth his steps.

Jimmy said, "By the end of the week, if you decide that you want to go back to Delaware, we will help you get home. But if you stay here you need to pull your weight."

I responded, "No problem, I am not afraid of hard work."

I want to take a praise break right here! MY GOD! Hallelujah! Glory to GOD in the Highest! It was just JESUS who was with me all the time! Do you hear me?

One of the songs in my repertoire was "The Blood" and I would sing that song all throughout the day to encourage myself. This song would bring me through time after time after time. "I know it was the Blood of JESUS that saved me, that kept me, that shielded me." This Earth-moving and shaking declaration will shift every atmosphere. Even though I was not walking in the will of GOD, I could feel HIS Grace and Mercy resting on me. Every time I called my mom before we ended our conversation, she would pray for me.

I was staying in a different state deep in the countryside with 16 to 18 men, whom I had just met. I could have been raped or killed, but GOD! Do you hear me? But "GOD favored me!"

I worked hard and the men grew to respect me because I did not allow anyone to carry my weight. I had to ride to and from the work site (tobacco field) in the bed of a pickup truck. Every day I determined in my mind to challenge myself to build up my stamina because I was going to sit in the front of that truck. Within two to three weeks, I was able to finish my row and to assist others. Now, keep in my mind that Jimmy had purposely placed me with a crew of older men, who were in their late 40s and early 50s. These were men who drank moonshine just about every evening. I was twenty-one years old and did not drink alcohol, so once my endurance and fortitude were intact I was a force to be reckoned with!

I opened a savings account and I saved more than half of my earning on a weekly basis. After the tobacco season ended, we had down time for almost a week. I decided to stay on to pick sweet potatoes. I might mention that I had started to date someone by this time. (I was operating in adultery.)

Well, one Sunday in October, my friend guy and I went out to eat. Afterwards, I called my mom and she informed me that my husband had called several times to speak to me. I asked my mom if she had told him I had not returned to Delaware. She said, "I told him I don't know where Shirlene is, but she is not here."

He stated to Mom, "Well, if I don't find her with your help, I am going to kill her when I do."

I said to my mom, "Please don't worry; I will be fine." Mom, you prayed, and GOD kept me.

At that very moment, I saw my husband step off a Trailway's bus. I hid because I was afraid, but my friend guy was not afraid. He asked my husband what he was looking for. My husband said, "I am looking for my wife!"

My friend guy stated, "She is right here with me!"

We walked all the way back to the migrant camp with my husband holding my left hand and my friend holding my right hand. This walk felt like forever, but neither would let go of my hand. Jimmy told my friend that he was not welcome today because my husband was back. He stated, "So you are going to leave now!" My husband and my friend fought; I was so afraid that one of them might kill the other. I got some of the guys who stayed on the camp; they came and broke the fight up. I sat up all night because I was not happy to see my husband and I was waiting for him to strike out and hit me. But of course he didn't because of all the people I had around who would protect me. The

39

next day, we left North Carolina and traveled by Trailway's bus to Jessup, MD. He was trying to beat me up on the bus and driver told him he could get off at the next stop if there were any further problems that day.

I am still encouraging somebody to wait on GOD for your husband/wife! Amos 3:3 KJV: Can two walk together, except they walk agreed?

I called my mom when I got settled in Maryland and of course she prayed.

My husband and I both worked in a restaurant for several months and I saved our money. Guess what? One day, I woke up and he was gone again with all the money. Several days later, my husband called; he was in Florida. He said, "I apologize, but I had to get out of there. I'm in Florida I want to you to come down in a few months." I continued to work and to save and one day I took the Trailway's bus to Tampa, FL.

This is a good place to stop, so I will. I continue to thank ABBA FATHER for a praying mother. GOD favored me and I am still here today! In my travels, I worked very hard and GOD continued to allow me to learn some very valuable life lessons. I am encouraging you, you, and you to take your hands off the situation and surrender it unto GOD. HE always has a way of escape planned for us, but when we are walking in the spirit of pride and disobedience the enemy will try to come in and sift us a wheat. Proverbs 16:18 KJV: Pride goeth before destruction, and an haughty spirit before a fall. Remember, pride keeps us going around and around in circles and tied to the spirit of bondage.

40

Please recognize that only GOD's plan is the absolute right plan for our lives. 2 Corinthians 2:14 KJV: Now thanks be unto GOD which always causeth us to triumph in Christ.

Shirlene's Acknowledgements:

I truly give all Honor and Glory unto Jehovah GOD, JESUS (MY LORD and SAVIOR) and the HOLY SPIRIT (MY COMFORTER and GUIDE).

I would like to thank my mom (Shirley E. Jones), who has always spoken life to me and my siblings (Apostle Randy, Cyndi, Tim, and Andrea).

I would be remiss if I did not mention my handsome son (Jerome Jr.), beautiful daughter (Jasmine), and five handsome grandsons (KajMere, Jerome III, Jeremy, Jerron, and Caelan).

I would like to thank the men and women of GOD who sowed Spiritual seed in my life (Apostles Ivory & Evelyn Hopkins; Pastors Roland & Angela Coon; Apostle Levin & Rose Bailey, also Bishop Ronald and Apostle Fay Richardson).

I would like to thank my wonderful co-authors!

In memory of my father (Frank Reginald Olivis Jr.).

Also, I want to recognize my stepmother (Joyce Olivis) and my siblings (Anna, Charlotte, and Frank III).

I cannot overlook my beautiful BFFs—Teresa Winstead-Finney and Delores Anderson.

A big thank you to the supporters of S.O. S.A.D. Outreach Ministry and The WORD Empowers.

Last but certainly not least my sister/friend (Dr. Kishma A. George); we have been cheerleaders for each other for the past 20 years! Blessings and More Grace to you, Purpose Pusher!!!

Meet author Shirlene Jones

Shirlene is a native of Delaware. She has an adult son and an adult daughter, also the Grandmom to five grandsons.

In 2008, GOD used Shirlene to birth out S.O. S.A.D. Outreach Ministry (Save Our Sons And Daughters); this ministry is founded upon scripture Matthews 6:33 and Luke 10:2. S.O. S.A.D. Outreach Ministry is a street ministry. I heard the voice of the FATHER in 2008 say, "It is time to take ME out of the box." The aim of this ministry is to assist in any capacity to stop the violence among Delaware's youth and young adults; to see souls saved. Under the umbrella of S.O. S.A.D. Shirlene has hosted numerous Back-to-School Celebrations for At-Risk youth and their families; the focus of the celebrations was Learning, Life, and Love! The celebrations always included an onsite cookout; a DJ playing Christian music; games, i.e. jump rope, hula-hoop, and African-American history trivia; a meal was provided with a blessing for the people and the food; everyone ate together, there was plenty of food and freshly made cupcakes/cookies. The families were served like royalty. Over the past ten years, S.O. S.A.D. Outreach Ministry has provided more than 700 Backpacks and other supplies. Also, S.O. S.A.D. has sponsored periodic food boxes; as a result, over 3500 lbs. of food has been given in the community.

Shirlene is an intercessor. She has hosted an Annual Women's Conference called "ARISE" because it is time for the Daughters of Zion to Arise! Shirlene is currently sharing the Word every Tuesday morning @ 7:00 a.m. on Facebook Live with "The WORD Empowers!" Shirlene has both an Associate and Bachelor's degree in the area of Sociology. She is a Certified Drug and Alcohol counselor and a LBSW. She has a varied background in the Human Services field: from Substance Abuse to Mental Health to Social Work. She is currently serving in the capacity of a senior social worker for the State of Delaware. Also, Shirlene has volunteered for several years at a Code Purple Women's (Homeless) Shelter.

Shirlene is an active member of Calvary Church in Dover. A motivational speaker and mentor, she is very passionate about seeing souls won for the Kingdom of GOD.

Her mottos are, "The Sky is our only Limit!" and "If you Love JESUS first and then you can Love People."

Shirlene has been recognized by the Delaware State News on a few occasions for S.O. S.A.D. Outreach Ministry. Also, Shirlene had an ad featured in the very first issue of K.I.S.H. Magazine in Fall 2012. She had a full-page article in K.I.S.H Magazine in Spring 2014. She has been noted in K.I.S.H. Magazine as a Top 25 Baby Doll World Changer in 2018.

Contacts:

Please feel free to reach out to Shirlene Jones on social media, or via email address at shirlenejones38@yahoo,.com

An Unexpected Crisis Can Become a Divine Appointment

By Wanda S. Briscoe

"I want you to know brothers, that what has happened to me has really served to advance the gospel." (Philippians 1:12 ESV)

Have you ever thought that maybe you should receive a warning before a crisis comes knocking on your door? Merriam Webster describes the word "crisis" as a radical change of a status in a person's life, an unstable or crucial time, or a state of affairs, in which a decisive change is impending. The definition sounds disheartening, but as a believer, we have to reflect on Romans 8:28 (NLT), which states, "And we know that God causes **_everything_** to work together for the good of those who love God and are called according to his purpose for them."

I have had to endure a lot of unexpected crises in my life, and when they showed up, I did not understand the "why" or the purpose. At times, I felt overwhelmed and frustrated. I am quite sure that you have felt the same way at times. Let me share a few examples of some unexpected crises I went through and how they turned into a divine appointment by the Lord.

On January 19, 2011, I received the unwanted telephone call from my doctor, and she said four tragic words, "You have breast cancer!" Those four words shook me to my core. It felt like someone had kicked me in the stomach, and I literally fell to the floor. I thought about my kids and my family. I thought, *Will I be cured? Will there be pain? How long will I live? How will my family handle this?* After I got myself together, it was as if I gained a supernatural strength, and I knew I had to get up off my floor and get myself together and fight. I had to fight for my life! This was an unexpected crisis, but I was not going to let it defeat me. I stood on the scripture in John 11:4. "This sickness is not unto death, but for the glory of God, that the Son of God might be glorified thereby." (KJV)

After I finished my multiple breast surgeries, and an extreme amount of radiation treatments, I did a self-evaluation, and I realized that breast cancer saved my life. I know that you are probably thinking, *Why in the world would she say that?* The crisis of breast cancer showed me that I was existing and not living. My relationship with God was not where it needed to be, but breast cancer brought me back to Him. After I would come home from my radiation treatments, I started writing in a journal on my breast cancer journey. The writings from this journal turned into me giving speeches at different churches across the country. Then, from giving speeches, soon thereafter, my first book, *The Fight Within*, was birthed. During my breast cancer journey, God gave me a scripture to mediate on, which is Isaiah 66:9 (NCV): "I will not cause pain without allowing something new to be born, says the Lord." It was a revelation to me, and it made sense as to why I had to go through my breast cancer journey. God was shaping me and molding me to be a voice to educate people on the life-threatening disease, to minister to women on the spirit of unforgiveness, and it pushed me to walk in my calling. From my unexpected crisis of breast cancer, my business called Mariposa Enterprises LLC was birthed, which supports the whole person (mind, body, and spirit) by providing them with educational information, community connections, and spiritual support as they are going through the entire cancer journey (diagnosis, treatment, and recovery). The global mission is to change the world's view of cancer.

Can you now see how an unexpected crisis can turn into a divine appointment? I am sure you have had some experiences that when you were going through them you did not understand the "why", but after God brought you through, you used that experience to become a better person. Have you ever thought that what we go through is not about us, but it is to help someone else? An unexpected crisis can allow dreams to be birthed within you. You may have dreamed of being an author, starting a business, being a community activist or more, but you did not have the "push" that you needed to step out on your faith. Maybe that crisis was the "push" you needed. Mark Twain has a quote that says, "The two most important days are the day you are born and the day you find out why." Could your expected crisis have been the day you found out why you needed to go through what you did, for you to do what God has called you to do?

Another example of an unexpected crisis that I went through truly blindsided me in the worst kind of way. In 2016, God gave me six words, "The Storm Has A Ministry Too," and I wrote them as a Facebook post. I did not know why God gave me those six words, but He usually will give me a title or a phrase to write in a magazine or a book years ahead of time.

In early 2018, I started writing another book, and I gave it the title *The Storm Has A Ministry Too*. I was looking forward to ending 2018 on a high note. December has always been my favorite month of the year because I love the magic of Christmas. I have always been fascinated by the Christmas lights, all the holiday decorations, the cooking, and spending time with my family. I never imaged in a million years that I was about to be hit with a telephone call that would drastically change my life forever. On December 3, 2018, I received a telephone call informing me that my youngest son had been shot and killed at the age of 22. This has been the biggest crisis that I have faced in my entire life. I did not get a warning that this crisis was about to happen, there were no signs from God, nor did a prophet give me a "word" for me to prepare. As the days of dealing with funeral arrangements passed, and when I was finally able to think, I did not ask God, "Why did this happen?" Instead, I asked Him, "What can I learn from this?" This crisis almost destroyed me emotionally and mentally as a mother. My faith was shaken, and most days it felt like I was walking through a thick fog.

I asked God to send people my way who had experienced losing a child to help me with the death of losing my son and people to help me to do something positive with my crisis, and

God honored my prayer. Even in your darkest hour, God will send help. I joined a national organization comprised of over six million volunteers nationally called Moms Demand Action for Gun Sense in America. I later became the Faith and Team Lead for the chapter in my county. I started speaking about gun violence and its impact in our community, especially among people of color. This crisis has started the conversation of parents discussing with their children the importance of being cautious about who their friends are. It started communication within the church that there must be real conversations regarding the tactics that the devil will use because if he cannot get to you, he will attack your bloodline. We cannot just quote scriptures and not know the culture of this wicked world; we must watch as well as pray. This crisis has given me an international platform on my Wanda's Warriors Live broadcast where mothers from all over the world send me messages to help them and to pray for them as they are coping with gun violence.

So, do you now see how God used my unexpected crisis of dealing with the murder of my son to advance the Gospel? Yes, it has been a bittersweet experience, but a lot of times, God will turn a tragedy into triumph. One of my favorite stories in the Bible is the story of Joseph. He was betrayed by his brothers, and he was thrown into a pit. To make matters worse, Potiphar's wife tried to seduce Joseph, and he refused her sexual advances, and she made a false accusation of rape. This was a hard crisis that Joseph went through, but in the end, God changed everything around, and Joseph was made a ruler in Egypt, second in line to the king.

Joseph was lied on and betrayed, but he never doubted God. Joseph was stripped of his precious coat of many colors, but he did not let that affect his character. That within itself is a lesson that we can learn when we are going through a crisis, and that is how our character speaks for us. How do you handle yourself when a crisis occurs? Do you blame God? Do you fall apart and give up when a crisis enters your life? How you handle an unexpected crisis can determine if you will keep repeating the same tests and trials. How do you handle yourself when you are lied on like Joseph and betrayed? I have had this happen to me, and it does not feel good. It hurts, and you want to go after the person or persons and to defend yourself. We have to let God handle the perpetrators, and a lot of times, God doesn't handle them immediately. Sometimes, He takes years to vindicate you, but trust me; it will happen. In the meantime, you keep serving God and doing His will. Keep doing what you were called to do to advance the gospel. The unexpected crisis of having your name scandalized does not feel good, and you have to hold your peace, but God can turn it around for His good.

Psalm 23:5 (in part): "You prepare a table before me in the presence of my enemies" is a scripture that I had to learn to rely on. Every crisis I have gone through that has tried to destroy me, every lie, and every betrayal, God has used those uncomfortable circumstances to further the Gospel. God has vindicated me right in front of my enemies, and given me platforms, and opened doors for me that I never dreamed of. He will do the same for you. You may not think that your crisis can elevate you, but keep trusting in God and He will turn things in your favor. God will get the glory in every crisis in your life if you keep trusting Him. Do not faint or get weary.

Use the journal to write down your various crises and date them. When God uses each of those crises to further advance the Kingdom, write it down. You will look back on your journal and marvel at your growth in God and how you handle your crises for it will all work out for your good.

Record Your Crises That Became Divine Appointments

_____

_____

_____

_____

_____

_____

_____

_____

_____

_____

_____

_____

_____

_____

_____

_____

_____

_____

_____

_____

_____

_____

_____

_____

_____

_____

_____

_____

_____

_____

_____

_____

_____

_____

_____

_____

_____

_____

_____

_____

_____

_____

_____

_____

_____

_____

_____

_____

_____

_____

_____

_____

_____

_____

_____

_____

Wanda's Acknowledgements:

To my Lord and Savior, Jesus Christ: I humbly "Thank You" for never giving up on me even at times when I wanted to give up on myself. You have prepared me for such a time as this, and I shall walk boldly in my calling and all that you have called me to be.

In loving memory of my youngest son, Darryl B. Dennis, II. You were tragically taken from us on December 3, 2018, but memories of your smile and your spirit keep me going. I have used this tragedy to help other mothers, and I know that you are so proud of me.

I am eternally grateful for my parents, Bishop John and First Lady Mary Ann Briscoe, for instilling in me at an early age the heart of a servant. I grew up as a child serving others and giving back to the community, and it is a part of my nature. There has not been a time when the both of you have not been there for me or for my sons. You are my spiritual covering as well as my natural covering, and I love you both dearly.

To my sons, Jarren and Jaquan, I continue to pray Psalms 91 over your lives, and I thank God for the amazing men that both of you have evolved into. I watch in awe to see the both of you starting your own families, and it makes my heart glad. I love you both to the moon and back.

To my amazing group of "pushers" (you know who you are), ya'll are the best! We started out as friends, but throughout the years, we have grown to be family. We pray for and with each other, we support each other, we congratulate each other, and we push each other to be all that God has called us to be. God knew who I needed in my life, and I love all of you.

A special "Thank You" to Dr. Kishma George, our divine connection happened in October 2019, and on that very day, you prophesied blessings into my life. I do not know what you saw in me, but I am thankful that God brought you into my life. By you giving God your "Yes," you are helping and pouring into so many people, and I am grateful for you.

Lastly, to all of my supporters who pray for me, who have purchased my products, who have supported my business and speaking platforms, thank you for believing and encouraging me. God has blessed me with the best Wanda's Warriors!

Always remember my motto and incorporate it into your life: Live ~ Out ~ Loud!

Meet author Wanda Briscoe

Wanda was diagnosed with breast cancer in 2011 and she was the first person in her family to be diagnosed with this life-threatening disease. Wanda did not see breast cancer as a death sentence, and she started educating others about the disease. She wrote her first book in 2012, called *The Fight Within*, which is about her breast cancer journey. In 2014, Wanda co-wrote a book called *The Art of Activation* with 23 authors from around the country. Wanda has had the opportunity to grace the cover of two magazines, (1) *Southern Maryland Women* and (2) *Gospel 4 U*, for her breast cancer awareness.

Wanda has received a special recognition letter from the former first lady Michelle Obama and Bishop T.D Jakes for her book *The Fight Within*. In 2018, Wanda launched her first business called Mariposa Enterprises, LLC., which assists people who have been diagnosed with cancer by providing them and their families with educational information, community connections, and spiritual support. Wanda released another book in May 2019 titled *The Storm Has A Ministry Too* and this book was turned into a stage play on October 10, 2020, in Waldorf, MD.

Wanda has been a radio guest on Washington DC's own *Butch McAdams*. She has also been a guest on the *Dr. Kishma George* radio show, which airs on iWorship 96. The 13th Annual Prayzefest Gospel Network recognized Wanda internationally, on September 19, 2020, in a virtual ceremony as she received the prestigious Deloris Malone Jordan "Victorious Woman" Award for her endurance and fight for breast cancer. Wanda is a co-author of another book project called *Inspired by Love*, which was released in February 2021.

On December 3, 2018, Wanda's youngest son was murdered in Atlanta, GA, at the age of 22. Due to this tragedy, she became active in the national organization Moms Demand Action for Gun Sense in America, which is comprised of over six million volunteers across the nation. Wanda is the Faith and Team Leader for the St. Mary's County, MD chapter of this organization.

In September 2019, Wanda became a radio host on WBGR Gospel Network, and her show was called *Wanda's Warriors*, but due to the COVID pandemic the show ended on the network in May 2020. Wanda re-launched the *Wanda's Warriors* show virtually on August 6, 2020 on Facebook and YouTube live, and she uses this platform to uplift the Kingdom of God, bring awareness to community issues, and promote small business owners. Wanda is a sought-after inspirational speaker and a mentor and she loves uplifting others by sharing her stories of triumph.

Wanda Briscoe ~ Contact Information

Address: 23415 Three Notch Rd, Suite 2008-109, California, MD 20619

Phone: 240-620-6447

Website: www.wandabriscoe.org

Email: wandaswarriors1@gmail.com

Facebook: https://www.facebook.com/wanda.briscoe

Instagram: https://instagram.com/iamwandabriscoe

Twitter: https://twitter.com/wandabriscoe

LinkedIn: https://www.linkedin.com/wandabriscoe

YouTube: https://www.youtube.com/channel/ UCLnTniTUYBlEpS7lBUXiH3Q

From the Projects to the Pulpit

By Julian Jones

Although my mother was an evangelist of a local Pentecostal church, I soon became a product of my environment. Raised in the projects I was introduced to drugs, money, and luxury at an early age. My family was known as the neighborhood drug dealers. It was normal for me to see my uncles buying different cars, living in different houses, and traveling extensively. As a young boy in the projects, I saw a lot and it was customary to see drugs and money on the kitchen table with different people coming in and out of my grandmother's house, my uncles' headquarters for their drug operation. This vantage point would be my birthing grounds for a turbulent future in the years to come.

My mother did her best to keep us in church, but I was heading down a path of rebellion. I got kicked out of every school I ever attended—elementary school, middle school, high school, and even alternative schools. I was in and out of juvenile detention centers. At the age of 14, my mom had to send me to live with my dad because she couldn't control my behavior. Staying with my father was short-lived because I could not handle the structure. I missed the freedom of living with my mother because with her I was able to come and go as I pleased and stay out as long as I wanted to.

It was at this age that my life began to take a turn for the worse, into a life of crime. I was introduced to sex, drugs, and an affiliation with a well-known gang. In order to join my new community, I had to prove I had heart; this required me to punch someone so hard that I knocked them out. The plan was for this to happen at our school football game. This initiation brought such an adrenaline rush, and I soon became addicted to violence and seeing people lying on the ground from the force of my hands.

My new family taught me how to fight, wrestle, dress, carry a gun, how to make money and talk to women. I felt respected, protected, and untouchable. I remember telling my mother, arrogantly, that I made more money than her.

By 15 I was breaking down pounds of marijuana on my mother's kitchen table while she was at work. One of these times my brother, who was a minister at the time, walked into the house and saw me packaging drugs. He told my mother what he had seen, and she didn't believe him because she always held on to the hope that I would someday be a pastor or a preacher. Even though she saw the people I hung out with and that I rarely came home, she was in denial about who and what I had become. Oftentimes she would walk into my room, pray for me and anoint my head with oil. I would be so aggravated because most times I would be high and drunk, but she never stopped praying for me. Of all my mother's four children I was her worst child.

By this time, I was no longer going to church; my mother had lost complete parental control of me. When I did go to church, I was selling weed to kids at church. So many times, I escaped near-death experiences. There's an old saying, you reap what you sow, and I was on the road to reaping a harvest that could cost me my life. We robbed people, broke into cars, and stole expensive stereo equipment not knowing that at some point we'd have to pay for the damage we were causing.

One night, a friend called and said they were looking for a pound of weed; the only issue was he lived on the other side of town, across the bridge. One of our rules was that we didn't go on the other side of the bridge, but because we knew the person and I trusted him we decide to fulfill this business transaction not knowing we were walking into an ambush.

We made our way out of the projects, across the bridge and our customer got in the backseat. He wanted to smoke a sample of what we were going to sell him. My best friend, who was on the passenger side, rolled up the weed and we smoked the whole blunt. We drove a block and come back.

He said, "Hey man, I only got half and I'm waiting on my homeboy to come with the rest of the money. If you want to, y'all can get out, come inside, and chill until he gets here."

I wanted this transaction to be over so I could go home, so I said, "Naw man, I'm cool. We gone stay in the car and hit another blunt."

He said, "Bet."

We hit another block and returned to the apartment. The guy came outside and told us his friend hadn't made it yet and that he was going to go back into the apartment to call him again. As we were sitting in the car, waiting, we noticed another man coming around from the back of the car from behind the projects.

As he got closer to the car he looked inside and said, "Hey, JuJu, is that you?"

I said, "Yeah man. What's up?"

He said, "Man, we were getting ready to rob you."

He recognized me because we went to school together and I was the father to his first cousin's baby.

He informed me that if we would have come inside the apartment, they had planned to cut the lights off and beat us with sticks and bricks. They were going to rob us. That was just one of many incidents where I escaped with my life.

The customary life of the streets causes you to become paranoid and you don't trust people. You're always looking over your shoulders when you're at the store, at school, and even in the club. We never went anywhere alone. There were always between two to 10 of us, we were always with somebody. As I moved up in influence and the ranks, I had to fight to keep my respect. I remember fighting a guy who was 6'4 and 264 pounds. He was a football player and a part of a well-known gang. He challenged me to a fight because he was trying to gain respect.

We had words in the hallway after the second period and I knew it was going to be trouble. As we stepped into our makeshift boxing arena, everyone crowded around us, the hallway was packed. I didn't want to fight, but I knew I had to because we now had an audience that was anticipating violence. He threw the first punch and it landed on my face. It stung, but when I saw that he didn't have the power to knock me out, I knew I could beat him. I busted his lip and nose and won the fight. Defeating a guy bigger than me who was a high-ranking member of a rival gang solidified my respect. After the 10th grade, I never had to fight anyone again; because of that one fight I was known as someone who had hands and power and was not to be played with.

Owning nice cars, dressing well, and hanging around some of the toughest and most well-respected guys in the city caused me to feel a sense of importance. When I went to school, my friends looked up to me, they respected me, and the young ladies loved me. By 17 years old I was the father of two kids with no blueprint of how to be a father because I didn't grow up with my own. To this day I don't know how I graduated from school. I believe the teachers allowed me to pass to the next grade because they didn't want to see me again.

As my drug clientele grew, family members began to sell drugs for me. I learned entrepreneurial skills at an early age, to organize and strategize in my neighborhood in order to sell out of my products.

At 16 I was able to enter clubs where the age requirement was 21 years old because of the lavish lifestyle I lived. Drugs and alcohol became a daily routine and that was the only way I could function. Although I had strayed away from the things my mother taught me, I felt like God never left me. I would have dreams of preaching in auditoriums and churches, but I told myself I would never be a preacher. I didn't want to be a preacher. I wanted my own club and to be the biggest drug dealer in my city. No matter how high I got, how much money I made, or how many women I had I felt empty on the inside. I knew I was called to do something special; I just didn't know what it was, all I knew was nothing fulfilled me, and I was consistently trying to fill this void. I thought the more I did the more the void would be filled, but nothing made it go away.

Of the main five guys in my circle, three of them went to jail, one was shot and killed, and for whatever reason God spared my life so many times. We would be sitting on the porch in the projects, shooting dice and smoking weed when the police would pull up and everybody would take off running. The police would chase us; we thought it was fun to outrun them. Looking back at that time, it was so dangerous; we could've been shot, but God protected us.

Getting high, selling drugs, and having multiple women wasn't enough, my newfound habit was gambling—shooting dice. I recall one Friday night I was at a dice party with other local drug dealers, it was an amazing night for me. It was a high-streak night, I won about $7,000. I took all these guys' money; some would leave to get more and then come back. I was so "hot" that I would give them back their money back just to win it back again.

The room was tense. I guess my friend could feel the danger lurking in the air because he leaned over to me and said, "Hey man, you need to leave or they're going to rob you to get their money back."

I could feel their anger and every now and then I would hear this voice echoing in my ear. *"You're going to die."*

I was enjoying the life of sin, but it was crazy to me that I would still have dreams about preaching. I would often rehash the mothers of the church patting me on my head at six and seven years old, calling me a little preacher and saying I would be a preacher someday. At this stage of my life, I thought, *No way. There is no way God could use someone like me.* From time to time, I would visit my mother's church, and no one would speak to me. They all knew what I did and that I was trouble, I guess the response should've been expected. I sat in the back of the building with all my jewelry on and I stayed through praise and worship, but when the preacher got up to preach, something would tell me to leave, and out I flew. I still carried a disdain for church people from the days of their judgment because we were project kids. They treated us differently, oftentimes they would prophesy to the kids whose parents had great jobs but never to us, the kids from the projects. At some point, it caused me not to like church because I knew they looked down on us. After all, we didn't dress like the other kids.

My friends and I lived for the weekend; we couldn't wait to get to the club and show off our latest Jordans, our jewelry, our women, and have a great time. But with the "show off" life comes great risk. There were always guys in the club looking for trouble. Shoot, sometimes we went to the club looking for trouble. In the midst of partying and showing off, the voice crept up to my ears. *"You're going to die."*

I believe it was my mother's prayers that kept me alive. One Friday night I will never forget, my boys and I were driving to a club in the middle of nowhere. I had this feeling that I should've stayed home, but I went anyway. I was fearless, I wasn't scared of anything. I got to the club and we were having a good time. I was waiting for my buzz from the weed I had smoked to kick in; that's when I would get loose and dance. This night, it was hot and jam-packed. There were different sets of gangs throwing up their gang signs during a song the DJ was playing. The mood turned violent, what started as fun turned into people pushing and shoving. Fights were breaking out from one side of the club to the other. I heard gunshots and people breaking bottles. I saw people picking up chairs and the sounds of metal chairs hitting heads and bodies falling to the ground. It was chaos. People were running out, forcing themselves through the only exit they had. The voice resounded in my ears again, *"You gone die tonight."* As I was running and fighting my way out of the club, a guy right beside me got hit with a bottle that someone threw across the dance floor. The bottle busted his head, and he fell to the ground unconscious. Somehow, I made it out without a scratch.

There were times I made it home from the club, drunk, and I found myself in the driveway of my home, not even remembering how I got there.

Around the age of 18, God started convicting my conscience more and more, different from the voice before, now it was saying, *"It's almost time."* I wasn't sure what it meant, but it was now haunting me in my sleep.

My stepfather never gave up on me and he would often say to me, "God's going to use you one day. You have to get saved and give your life to Him."

My routine response was, "I can't. I don't even have a mind to be saved."

He would follow up with, "Pray and ask God to give you a mind to be saved."

Then, finally, one day I got tired of the routine. I was exhausted with getting high first thing in the morning, making illegal money, hanging with women, and doing the same thing every day, over and over. The feeling that there was something special I was supposed to do wouldn't leave me.

I woke up one morning after a night at the club, I had a hangover and felt drowsy. I had the worst headache and at that moment I realized something *had* to change. In all my mess, I simply asked God to help me. I didn't know that would be the beginning of change. After that prayer, it didn't matter how much weed I smoked I couldn't get high and when I would drink, I would get sick. God began to take the taste for smoking weed and alcohol out of my mouth.

I remember like yesterday when my life shifted again. It was family day at my church and my dad asked me if I would be his guest at service. I had a new three-piece suit I had never worn. My mother bought it for me to attend church. I figured family day would be as good a time as any to wear my new suit. To add the cherry on top I had a beautiful new girlfriend who was a college student. I was just a senior in high school; of course I had to bring her to church to show her off.

What I hadn't anticipated was that this Sunday would be the beginning of my transformation. I pulled up in my nice car and walked inside the service with my lovely date on my right arm. I felt important. That Sunday, the power of God began to move; young people were getting saved and filled with the Holy Ghost with the evidence of speaking in tongues. I didn't know what was going on, but whatever they had, I wanted it. It was powerful, the anointing was so strong. I saw young people running to the altar to be saved. Tears were flowing down my face. I felt the presence of Almighty God. I heard the voice, again, God's voice, say to me, *"It's time. Today is your day."*

I asked the lady in front of me if she would walk down to the altar with me for prayer. Trembling, I reached the altar; the pastor laid his hand on my head and he said, "God said today is your day." At that moment, my life changed.

He asked me if I wanted to be saved. I said yes and he prayed for me and then they took me to the back to be baptized.

I had on a thick 14-karat gold necklace and a gold rope necklace; I snatched them off and yelled, "Devil, I'm giving you back all your tools!"

I was baptized that very night, in the name of Jesus Christ. As I was delivering my life over to Christ and I emerged from the water, I heard people shouting and yelling with excitement, some praying for me and encouraging me. I walked back to my seat through the rejoicing crowd. My girlfriend looked at me shocked and asked, "What does this mean?"

I responded with, "The things I used to do I can't do anymore."

My transformation process wasn't easy because the people in the church were waiting for me to backslide. Six months after I was baptized, an elder in the church came up to me with disbelief and said, "You still hanging in there. I didn't think you would make it long." That was heartbreaking.

There was one man of God, Elder Perry, every Sunday, he would encourage me saying, "Hang in there." He knew I was fighting. My friends, my teachers, and even my family were shocked. I was outlasting all their tragic expectations of me.

Working a regular job was different, living a normal life had its challenges. My best friend, my partner in life, came to my house one day and laid a load of cash on my bed with drugs and told me to get back in the game.

I looked at him and said, "I want to be saved, I'm not going back." My mind was made up. I couldn't go back. I knew there were a lot of people waiting for me to fail; that alone built my determination to stay the course.

My dreams of preaching continued intensifying. At 19 years old, on a Sunday morning on my way to church, I heard God say, *"Feed my sheep. Feed my sheep."* I didn't know it at the time, but that was a passage in the Bible. I immediately told my pastor what God kept saying to me and that I wasn't sure what it meant. He told me it meant God was calling me to preach.

At 19 I accepted my calling to preach, and I preached my first sermon at 21, the title of the message was *Don't Look Back*. I

preached at a youth service by default because the guest preacher
didn't show up and my pastor looked at me and said, "You're
preaching tonight."

That night, the power of God fell on me as I administered
the Word of God, it seemed as though I had been preaching my
entire life. It felt good. As I began to release the Word of God it
was the first time that I could hear Him clearly speaking in my
ear and I was trying to release it as quickly as He released it to me.
As I preached God moved throughout the congregation. People
were praising Him, and some came to the altar to give their life
to God, it was such an amazing feeling to be used to by Him.
Amid my happiness and walking in my calling I also experienced
disappointments. I could tell some people were encouraged and
happy for me, but some weren't.

I wanted to be used by God. I fell in love with prayer and reading
my Bible. I wanted to learn so much more about God. I was like
a sponge. At the age of 23, I had a desire to go to Bible college.
Once again, my life was about to shift. The assistant presiding
over our church organization called my pastor and offered me
a partial scholarship to the Bible college I wanted to attend. My
pastor, who previously had doubts about me attending, permitted
me to attend Bible college with one request, when I moved back
I wouldn't start a church. At that time pastoring a church wasn't
even a part of my mindset, I just wanted to learn more about
God. Moving from the South to the Midwest and living in a
dorm with other young preachers from all over the country was a
culture shock. I didn't know this would be a moment that would
build brotherhood and would change the way I saw ministry for
the rest of my life.

The entire time God was strategically developing me and ordering my steps to fulfill the dream I kept having from a young boy to a teenager, to a young adult. After extensive years of biblical studies and traveling as an evangelist I knew God was calling me to more. I was fortunate to have an amazing example of preaching while watching my pastor, Bishop Lambert Gates Sr., shepherd his congregation. It was an experience I'll never forget, he was a builder and an encourager, and, in some ways, it made me who I am today. I watched everything he did. I experienced up close the epitome of a pastor, the way he loved, nurtured, and cared for the people of God.

Once again, I heard that voice. *"Feed my sheep. Feed my sheep."* God was still dealing with me about pastoring. I was so nervous when I sent my bishop an email requesting a meeting to share with him what God was impressing upon me. I didn't know what to expect or even if he would believe me. To my delight, he encouraged, blessed, and released me into my ministry. It was such a relief. I felt like God was calling me to move back home to start a church. There were so many friends from high school, in my family, and in my community that were lost, and God had given me a unique burden for the city I once grew up in.

I was wrestling deep down inside about being a pastor and I remember telling God, "Nobody is going to believe that You called me to be a pastor." People can love you as an evangelist but have a hard time accepting you as a pastor.

God spoke to me that night and reassured me with, *"They didn't believe in Jesus and they called Him Beelzebub. Feed my sheep."*

In my pursuit to obey God, I was gripped with fear, I questioned Him. I was like Moses, giving God excuses. I reminded God of my plight and that I was unmarried, but He reminded me of His instructions to *Feed His sheep*. This new faith and hearing God's voice made me courageous. I didn't know where to start or what to do, I had no money, but I decided to walk by faith, and I started looking for a building. I didn't know how I would purchase a building or even when, but I had a dream from God.

I contacted some people about renting out a plaza to host the church. I had no members, just faith. They told me that there were other churches interested in the building, but they assured me they would get back to me. To my surprise, the lady called me the next day and said, "I don't know why, but God is telling me to help you." She even gave us our first month free. That day, Judah Life Christian Center was born. We started with five people and in one year we grew to 100 people. We eventually outgrew the plaza and moved into a 37,000-square-foot facility; our membership expanded. We started a child development center that grew from nine kids to 60 kids on average.

It finally dawned on me one Sunday morning in my new office at the church, after all those years of living a life many would only watch on TV, that the dream I had as a boy, as a teenager, and as a young adult ...I was living in it.

I want to conclude with this: your dream is a glimpse of your destiny, who you're going to become. Your dream is God speaking to you about your future. Like Joseph who saw himself being in the palace but didn't know he'd have to go through a pit to get there. We will all travel through a Joseph experience, just as I did going from the projects to the pulpit.

Julian's Acknowledgments

I would like to give a huge thanks to my parents, my mother Kimberly Hogan and my father Wedlow Jones Jr. Thank you for everything!

Special thanks to the greatest Pastor I know, Bishop Lambert Gates Sr., Pastor of Mount Zion Apostolic Church, your care, character, and consistency to represent Christ well impacted my life in ways I'm striving to become daily.

Thank you to Anesha Sharp for your help and assistance with the book.

To the wonderful church I pastor, Encounter Christian Church. Thank you!

And last but certainly not least, I want to give thanks to the Lord and Savior of my life, Jesus Christ!

Meet author Julian Jones

Julian Jones is the senior pastor of the second church plant, Encounter Christian Center in Nashville, TN. He is also an entrepreneur, mentor, life coach, author, ministry consultant, and prophet to the nations. He has a passion for evangelism and outreach. "For the Son of man is come to seek and to save that which was lost." Luke 19:10

Rejection Is a Set-Up

By Dale Broome

"You have not been accepted into the Executive MPA program at..."

T didn't hear another word as I stared at the first line of the rejection letter, as if doing so would change the words on the paper. They remained the same! I had not been accepted into the Executive Master of Public Administration program at this Ivy League school as I had hoped. With a 3.92 current graduate-level GPA, I had sought a transfer into the university's Executive MPA program and was quickly offered an interview upon my application. Surely it was a done deal, I thought, with my overconfident self. Power-suited and dressed for success, I prematurely exited the train following the erroneous advice of a total stranger, rather than using the directions I had carefully researched. I knew better!

It was the walk from hell, having to walk block after block in the scorching heat, in my high heels, turning up to the school like a drowned rat. With my suit soaked and my hair drenched, everything was clinging to me as if in a wet-shirt competition. Thank God that out of an abundance of caution I had caught an early train, giving myself an additional two hours of wiggle room, in the event of a delay. I made a beeline for the nearest bathroom and made the paper towels my personal bath towel. Restored to my elegant self, I confidently sauntered my way towards the interview room.

Alas, there was more heat in store for me as I was grilled like a burger by an elderly gentleman with cold eyes and an absent smile. The interview, or shall I say the discouragement session, lasted approximately forty-five minutes. As I excitedly told the gentleman about my book and the organization I had founded to help young males succeed–he seemed unimpressed. Juvenile Justice Reform was one of my selling points. His exact words to me were, "What make you think that you can succeed where others have failed? There is no hope for those boys you want to help!" he added with a hint of scorn. I humbly submitted to him that perhaps those who failed were in the wrong lanes—that is, the wrong callings. His eyes remained arctic.

As I stared at the apologetic wording of the rejection letter, I realized that this was just another notch on a lengthy belt of rejection. As I felt rejection beginning to set in like gangrene, I asked the Lord again, "Why did you let me waste my time?"

I heard the spirit of the Lord clearly, "Rejection is just a set-up for my Glory to be seen in you." As I pondered on what that meant, the next words were just as clear. "The Ivy League will not take credit for where I am taking you."

I was taken back to many years of rejection—most of it in the workplace—being overlooked repeatedly for over two decades. My rejection journey had been a long, painful process. So much that I placed the following declaration over my head, where I could see it every day in my workspace. Printed in bold and highlighted in hot pink, there is no missing it. "The stone which the builders rejected, the same is become the Head of the corner." This is a constant reminder that Jesus Himself was rejected, but He became the "chief cornerstone" (Matthew 21:42; Psalm 118: 22, NKJV). I had to allow God to take me through the process to get to my victory. Like a pregnant woman going through a painful delivery, knowing she must push her way through to her bundle of joy, giving up was not an option for me. My spiritual muscles had to be developed and strengthened.

As I took a stroll down Memory Lane, I remembered quite vividly one of countless interviews I had for top management positions at my workplace. On this particular day, I was called into "the office" for my "Rejection tête-à-tête," which was typically scheduled just before the close of day on a Friday evening. This allowed an employee to sulk over the weekend and return to work the Monday 'recovered' and 'refreshed' from the disappointing news. Later, upon comparing the rejection explanations amongst one another, the reasons exchanged were typically inconsistent, conflicting, and faux. On this particular occasion, in the explanation for not being given the position (again), I was told the following: "You don't need this job; you are better off with those at-risk boys you like to help." Having utilized my lunch hours and vacation time to attend board meetings, my volunteer activities were no secret to those in the workplace. I had grown so accustomed to being denied that I wasn't even shocked by the words, just sad.

In retrospect, those words did play a part in helping to catapult me into the birthing of the non-profit organization, Destination Greatness, which was founded primarily to help at-risk boys succeed. In fact, our name is our destination!

I remember another time waiting to be interviewed for another position—this time a lower managerial position. Each department had a manager and a supervisor, and my manager had relocated to another state, leaving the position vacant. Interestingly enough, I had been her supervisor when she was a case manager. When the management position had become vacant, she was placed in the position, making her my manager instead. I felt like I had been slapped in the face and really cried out to God about the unfairness of it all, especially since this wasn't the first time something like this had happened to me. Years previously, I had assumed the duties of director of my department for a very long time and then watched as it was given away to someone else.

Now here we were back to square one with this manager position available once again. Being next in line, I, of course, applied for the position and watched as it stayed vacant for approximately a year while I acted in the position managing my department. I was given a "heads-up" that those in authority wanted someone else for the position. Well, I soon found out my fate. I was called into "the office" shortly thereafter and told that the position would not be filled after all. Instead, the entire department was going to be closed down and my staff bifurcated to two other managers.

What came next was like another slap to my invisibly flushed face. The exact words were, "Which leaves us with what to do with you. You don't need to be a supervisor. You have so many skills. You write so well! You can research a thing to death! We have projects for you to do!»

Can I tell you that was over twelve years ago and I am still working on the same project? Once the project was implemented and the initial kinks worked out, I did not move on to any other project as led to believe. Always striving to excel at whatever I do, I was basically forgotten. The famous words "Set it and forget it" are permanently embedded in my brain.

At one point in my reflections, I realized I had gone from exclusively managing murder cases for seventeen years, interstate detainer cases, welfare fraud cases (along with supervising a staff of criminal case managers ranging from the arraignment process to the trial process) to being thrust into sub-level tasks way beneath my God-given potential. Such tasks included cutting out heads from "passport-style" photos daily and gluing them on cards; then individually laminating hundreds and hundreds of gun permits. Please know that there is absolutely nothing wrong with humble beginnings, but I had already "paid my dues."

Boss Day, following my department being closed, was the worst! There was a time when each time I spoke about that day, tears and snot would compete down my face. But I can talk about it now because God has delivered me. I am free! He has dried my tears and healed my heart. I have forgiven those who hurt me repeatedly because I realize that they did not and still do not realize what they did. I pray that if there is any residue lurking within me, God will uproot it with the therapy this chapter brings. The Word of God states, "But I say to you, love your enemies, bless those who curse you, do good to those who hate you and pray for those who spitefully use you and persecute you" (Matthew 5:44, NKJV). Love, therefore, is the only option!

Back to that day; I was pretty much forgotten. I was not seen as a subordinate because I still had my title as supervisor. Neither was I seen as a superior because I no longer had any no staff reporting to me. Needless to say, my name was not on either of the two emails distributed to the two groups of staff members about an upcoming luncheon being prepared. This luncheon was to be prepared by subordinates, for bosses. I was going to be left in that office all by myself had it not been for a colleague/friend of mine who saw me and asked me if I wasn't going «upstairs.»

When I asked, "Upstairs where?" she asked me if I hadn't read my email. Like a scene from the movie *Clueless*, I then asked, "What email?" Having seen firsthand all that I suffered throughout the years, she felt my pain and went on a mission to get the oversight rectified. By the time the inadvertency was acknowledged, and I got to the location where the luncheon was being held, all the bosses had finished eating and had risen from their tables. Someone apologetically thrust a small gift bag in my hand, which was meant to give me some measure of solace. It didn't!

The rejection continued! I was cut from staff meetings, cut from staff attendance lists distributed daily to managers/supervisors, important emails, changes in office procedures, etc. I had to find out office information from others who heard it from feedback from their managers/supervisors and told me. I was totally left out of the loop. As I interviewed for some management positions externally, one of the leading questions would be, "How many employees do you manage?" I would then have to awkwardly explain that I no longer managed people but managed a project instead. I was always asked to explain what I meant by that. I would see the looks exchanged amongst the interview panel. Basically, the explanation did not fly! With the title Supervisor, the panel was expecting me to supervise people with pulses, not a project. It hampered my every move to get management positions outside of my office. I had tons of interviews, great interviews, great prospects, but nothing materialized. Nothing!

For many years, I found myself stuck in this same place—this corner. Though my knowledge, experience, and writing skills were drawn on repeatedly and conveniently, I was kept "in my place" with a succession of menial tasks and overwhelmingly tedious data entry that was primarily "the project." I became a one-man "assembly line." I was not only the "problem solver" but became the sole "workhorse" of this ever-evolving, multi-layered process. I found myself working late at night and coming in on weekends just to survive the tsunami of tasks threatening to push me under.

I was more determined than ever not to give up. I finally returned to my previous graduate program—Master's in Administration of Justice/ Leadership and Administration—finishing strong and was inducted into the Criminal Justice Honor Society. Graduation day was a proud moment for me with my symbol of honor—a heavy golden medallion swinging from a bright gold-and-blue ribbon around my neck. My children and my two best friends were in attendance to capture the moment on video. "Go put that master's degree to work" was the encouragement from co-workers and friends who cheered me on after viewing the video on social media.

Alas... Even with an advanced degree, with honors, nothing came through for me! I watched others younger and with less experience and education "moving on up" like the Jeffersons. I was struggling financially with no pay raises for almost a decade, yet the cost of living continued to go up like an Easter kite. Today, with twenty-eight years of service, with twenty of those years with the same title, I still am nowhere near the midpoint of my salary range. Yet others are already there from the day of hiring. In fact, I recently came across a paycheck statement from January 2007. I shook my head as I realized that my take-home pay was fifty-nine dollars ($59) less than a paycheck statement for March 2021 (fourteen years later).

I remember saying to the Lord, "Something has to give soon, Lord! Otherwise, I am going to crash and burn!" Meanwhile, I continued to volunteer my time and talent creating countless resumes and "State Minimum Qualifications" to help countless people (including employees) get where they belonged in the job market. I watched with joy as they got new jobs or got promoted, yet I couldn't seem to help myself. I wasn't going anywhere! As I watched people who didn't know or serve the Lord advance, my faith wanted to waver. I would constantly ask the Lord, "When, Lord? When is my turn?"

Originally from a foreign country, I felt like I was on the outside looking in! And even though I did not appear so outwardly, I felt like a total failure. Behind the smile and the designer outfits and shoes God continually used others to bless me with, nobody knew my struggles except those in my immediate circle. I couldn't help but think back to my career as a police officer in Barbados. With training as far as the D.E.A., F.L.E.T.C, Glynco, Georgia, I had passed the police exam and had been waiting to be promoted to sergeant when I had left the ranks. I know I would have risen through the ranks in my own country like my colleagues did. Every now and then, I wondered, *Did I make a mistake, Lord?* Regret would start to raise its ugly head, but not for long, as I became keenly aware of what God said; I was uprooted and transplanted to this country on purpose—for purpose! To impact the lives of many! I would hear the Lord saying, "For a moment, I have caused people to ride over your head, my daughter. You went through the fire and through the water, but I am bringing you out into a wealthy place (Psalm 66:12, KJV).

I am taken back to a service I attended in 2009, where the Man of God, all the way from Ghana, was praying for the people after the Word went forth. When he got to me, he looked me straight in the eyes and one of the things he said to me was, "God says you are made to feel like a doormat in the workplace, but He is going to change that." His words hitting that tender place in my heart caused the tears and the snot to flow like a fountain. He then spoke to the multiple gifts God has placed in me, ending with, "Ms. Wealthy Businesswoman! Ms. Wealthy Entrepreneur!" At the time, I was feeling far from it but knew enough about prophecy to know that it was for an appointed time. He was speaking into my future! He was speaking to the potential in me! He was calling those things forth that be not as though they were (Romans 4:17, NKJV). I left the service holding on to those words, feeling a sense of hope for the future. Just as I am feeling as I write today! Hope is alive!

I keep hearing in my spirit yet another prophecy. "You will be what some will call ... a late bloomer!" Back then, as I started to ponder what that meant, the explanation came. "All the things people typically accomplish in their earlier years will start coming to you in the latter half of your years." I still have those notes!

As the years flew by, I would ask the Lord, "How late, Lord? My gosh! When?"

As I kept whining to the Lord about not having enough, I kept hearing these words everywhere I turned: "What's in your hand? Use it! Everything you need is right there in your hands." It took a while for these words to resonate in my spirit. The Lord reminded me of the business, FAVOR that He had given me for years, but I continued to use it like volunteer work. "It is a stream of income," He said. "Use it! I WILL TELL YOU WHO TO BLESS!"

From the very beginning, I was asked by the court administrator, "Were you an English major? You write very well." This was the first in a succession of affirmations. I started to explain to people that it was my "British-influenced educational upbringing," but God corrected me. He said it was a special gift—a scribal anointing that He has deposited in me, for purpose! I am so careful now to give Him the credit. My writing gift was utilized in twenty-eight combined years of serving on boards championing the causes of Delaware's at-risk children and youth. Serving simultaneously as secretary on two boards of directors for many years, my writing gift was stretched to the maximum. Everyone used it and benefited from it freely, except me.

As I write this chapter, the resume business has now been relaunched along with a women's business clothing and accessories boutique. From as far back as Barbados, I have always believed in dressing for success. It doesn't matter if it doesn't look like it! Success is coming! My sister, Syntyche, a financial genius, knew of this dream and would encourage me every time I spoke about it to start with what I had. She would encourage me to take pictures, post them online and start building revenue. "Start small," she would say, "then you can get your building. I will help you!" As a financial advisor, I think she has always felt for me after seeing one of my paychecks. She was as appalled as I was embarrassed. "You are way too talented and smart to be making this meager amount of money, Dale."

After twenty-eight years of careful observation, I look around my workplace and see the disparities in hiring practices, salaries, workloads, and promotions, and I want to weep. In a system that should be the epitome of fairness and justice; where fairness should extend to every artery of that system—including support staff, there is dire need for an *independent* review and overhaul. I pray God exposes all workplace injustices everywhere!

I hear myself saying daily, "This is it! You have to get out of here, Dale! You have to get out of this corner! You have to get out of this cramped, box-laden eyesore of a cubicle, Dale! You have to come out of Lo-Debar! (2 Samuel 4, NKJV). You have to stop camping out along this brook that has dried up! (1 King 17: 8-16, NKJV). You have to fight for your promise, Dale! You have to believe what the Lord told you a long time ago: 'I have given you the ability to operate at the *pentagon* level.' You have to operate at that level, Dale! Get up! Get up! Get Up!"

So, I say to myself, "No more operating at a sub-standard level, accepting the crumbs from the table, Dale! The dreamer in me is rising with power!"

I've gone through the process—the long, difficult pregnancy—years and years of rejection. I've gone through the stripping, the humbling, and the rejection. I could have been one hateful, bitter, resentful, angry black woman, but instead, the joy of the Lord is my strength! The Word of God states in James 1:2 (NKJV) to "count it all joy when you fall into various trials, knowing that the testing of your faith produces patience." I've already asked the Lord to forgive all the people who rejected and oppressed me for years, especially those "pharaohs" in the workplace who, like the children of Israel under the hard taskmasters, ignored and continue to ignore each cry I made for help.

Because of "whose" I am, I was able to go through gracefully. It has all been preparation for my purpose! A set-up for the best-selling book(s) God is birthing in me! A set-up for the nonprofit He has birthed out through me to help others. A set-up for the billion-dollar enterprise He has given me to be a blessing to many; a set-up for my mentoring program for women who have experienced rejection just like me—those in the workplace who are daily made to feel less than! Those who are oppressed, suppressed, neglected and black-listed for speaking up against wrong! Those who are misunderstood, marginalized, and maligned! It's a set-up for the evangelist in me to burst forth! For out of my belly will flow rivers of living water (John 7:38, KJV). My God! It's a set-up for the Deborah anointing on my life!

A few years back, the Lord installed His vessel into a position to start the process of redeeming me from the hopelessness and despair I was feeling. He restored my dignity as a supervisor/manager. With at least one subordinate under my belt, I was invited back into activities that I had been excluded from. I knew it was God wanting to heal my emotions from workplace trauma, hurt and disappointment. I am truly grateful. This angel has since moved on, but even the latest rejection recently for another top management position could not faze me. I know that MY Redeemer lives! I know that I know that I know that it is God who is closing all the doors that need to be closed and opening those that need to be opened in this season. All the years of, seemingly, workplace unfairness is a set-up for that special desire God has placed in my heart.

Like Joseph, it's a set-up! Like me, Joseph sat seemingly stuck! He sat in prison while his talents and dreams, though known, were underutilized and suppressed. They were seemingly wasted and forgotten. But, at the right time, the Dreamer in him burst forth. The untapped potential in him was unleashed when the chief cupbearer finally remembered his gift and referred Joseph to Pharaoh. He was immediately summoned from the prison to the palace. As in Proverbs 18:16 (NKJV), his gift made room for him and brought him before great men! In this case, it brought him before King Pharaoh who needed what he had—the gift of interpreting dreams. This God-given gift caused him to be promoted to second-in-command of Egypt (Genesis 41, NKJV). But it was all in God's timing! Not a minute sooner! If God did it for Joseph, surely He can do it for you and for me!

Can I tell you that when the anointing of the Lord is on your life, you can't stay hidden forever? They better be careful where they throw you! In God's timing, NO devil in hell will be able to stop the hand or plan of the Lord on yours or my life. "For I know the plans I have for you," declares the Lord, "plans to prosper you and not to harm you, plans to give you hope and a future" (Jeremiah 29:11, NIV). Amen! I choose to take the Lord at His Word and give birth to my bundle(s) of joy! How about you?

I am here to declare that my "bringing out" is here! It's not a bad thing after all—being in the valley for over two decades. I am going to the mountaintop! For I hear the Lord saying, "In this season, I'm causing you to rise from the corner man has placed you in, with power from on High! Arise, My daughter, arise! Like the multifaceted task you have endured for years, I am awakening and calling forth the multifaceted Dreamer within you!" Amen!

May God's name be glorified and amplified in EVERY aspect of my life. I shall forever give Him Honor and the Highest Praise, for He is worthy! Amen and Amen!

Dale's Acknowledgements

First and foremost, I want to thank God who is the Head of my life. To Him and Him alone be all the Honor and the Glory given.

Next, I want to thank my late parents, Neville and Barbara Broome, who brought me up in the fear and admonition of the Lord, setting the Godly foundation for where I am firmly planted today. Never will I forget those mandatory 5:00 a.m. wake-up calls for prayer and family devotion around the dining room table with my six siblings. As the Bible states, train up a child in the way he should go, and when he is old, he will not depart from it (Proverbs 22:6, KJV). I will see you both in heaven.

Special thanks to my awesome siblings, my two sons, and my immediate family for their constant loving support. You are the best family a girl could ever ask for and have. May God bless each one of you exceedingly abundantly above all that you ask or think according to Ephesians 3:20, KJV.

Thanks to the board and volunteers of Destination Greatness Inc., and coaches, parents, and players of Destination Greatness Elite Basketball. Thank you for your support and believing in the vision.

Thanks to all the God-assigned friends God placed in my life over the years. Know that I love you. Screaming thanks to my BFFs, Margaret and Deirdre. You two have been there for me and my boys through the good, the bad and the extremely ugly. Thanks for your unconditional love, prayers, and never-ending support.

Thanks to all those who helped to push me into Purpose and Destiny. God knows your names!

Finally, to all my co-workers past and present, who suffered and continue to suffer in silence. It's time to arise! Time to come out of your corners everywhere! God has heard your 911 call for help. Help is on the way! I am declaring and decreeing that this is your "coming out" season! It starts today! Arise, Shine! For your light has come! And the Glory of the Lord is risen upon you (Isaiah 60:1, NKJV). Amen!

Meet author Dale Broome

Dale hails from the beautiful island of Barbados, where she served as a police officer in Drug Enforcement. She currently resides in New Castle County, Delaware and is currently employed with the Delaware Judiciary, where she has faithfully served the citizens of Delaware for twenty-eight (28) years. She is active in causes that improve the lives of children and youth in crisis, providing them with hope for a better life. Besides chairing the board of directors of Destination Greatness Inc., Dale has served on leading Delaware Boards for over twenty-eight years.

Dale is the founder of Destination Greatness, Inc., a 501(c)(3), Christ-anchored ministry of Restoration and Hope for males thirteen to twenty-six. She is also the founder of Destination Greatness Elite (Basketball), which is geared primarily towards exceptional and talented boys who are overlooked yearly at high school tryouts or selected but made to sit on benches watching their teammates play. The goal is to restore Hope and Encouragement as well as to unleash the UN-tapped potential within them, causing them to shine locally, nationally, and internationally. Both ministries are a piggy-back of her book, *Destined for Greatness: It's as Easy as Getting Back on the Bus,* which was published in 2012.

Part of Dale's educational history includes a Master's degree in the Administration of Justice/ Leadership and Administration from Wilmington University in Delaware, with Honors, where she was inducted into the National Criminal Justice Honor Society. She also holds a bachelor's degree in Criminal Justice from Widener University, Pennsylvania, where she was elected "Who's Who Among Students in American Universities & Colleges" by Widener University. Additionally, Dale has completed a graduate-level Executive Certificate program at Georgetown University, Washington, DC, in Nonprofit Management, at its Center for Public & Non-Profit Leadership.

Dale is also the visionary behind FAVOR, an upcoming Resume Consulting & Career Services business as well as its subsidiary—Barb's Closet, a business clothing and accessories boutique.

In 2018, Dale was honored to be spotlighted in the "Dynasty of Dreamers" column of *K.I.S.H. (International) Magazine* - March 2018 issue. Prior to that, in 2016, she was selected as one of four honorees at the Live on Purpose, "Be Bold; Be Beautiful" Awards Dinner, honoring BOLD and beautiful women who exemplified a spirit of BOLDNESS in family, faith, business and/or ministry. Shortly thereafter, Dale was again humbled to be honored by Empowered Women Ministries as 2016's "Empowered Woman of the Year," for Educational Advancement.

On a spiritual note, Dale has said "Yes" to the Global Evangelistic/Prophetic calling on her life. As a rising Deborah, her purpose is twofold: JUSTICE and LIGHT. She carries a heavy anointing to break the shackles of hopelessness and despair from the oppressed and the downtrodden and to set the captives free as mandated in Isaiah 42 and Isaiah 61. To this end, she recently founded Beautiful Feet Global Evangelistic Ministries (BFGEM) and its ancillary ministry, Oasis Ministries (Mentoring program).

Before elevating to BFGEM, Dale was a faithful member of Perfect Will Ministries (DE), for fifteen years. She is a member of the sisterhood of Daughters of Esther Ministry, Daughters of Zion, Sisters Empowering Sisters and the Gleaming Dreamers.

Contact information

DaleBroomeGlobal.com

info@DaleBroomeGlobal.com

Beautiful Feet Global Evangelical Ministries

Oasis Ministries (Mentoring)

Destination Greatness Inc.

https://DestinationGreatnessDE.com

DestinationGreatness@gmail.com

Destination Greatness Elite (Basketball)

DestinationGreatnessElite@gmail.com

FAVOR

https://favorbusinessenterprises.com

info@FavorBusinessEnterprises.com

Young Ladies of Excellence & Elegance (YLEE)

YLEE@FavorBusinessEnterprises.com

Barb's Closet (boutique)

BarbsCloset@FavorBusinessEnterprises.com

Dale.Broome@gmail.com

Facebook: https://www.facebook.com/dale.broome.524/

Instagram: @dale_broome

Processed for the Promise

By Ayanna Lynnay

ecently I saw a meme that said something to the effect of, "If your dreams don't scare you they are too small." I quickly liked that status and said, "Amen," but then I stopped and thought about it. Many of us will agree with that statement, but how many of us believe it and then do something about it? I have found with myself and talking with many others that dreaming big is usually not the problem; it is the execution and bringing it into physical manifestation that is difficult. Many of us give up and throw in the towel before we see the manifestation. We fail to realize that just because God has told us what He wants to do in our life it does not mean we just sit back idly doing nothing and wait for it to manifest. Oh no! There is WORK to do and a process to go through.

One of my favorite scriptures is 1 Corinthians 2:9: *However, as it is written: "What no eye has seen, what no ear has heard, and what no human mind has conceived" the things God has prepared for those who love him.* I truly believe that our blessings have already been prepared for us and the reason we have not obtained them yet is because God is preparing *us* for them. This is why it is so important to keep moving forward, to not throw in the towel and not to get weary in well doing because the Bible promises we will reap (see a return on all that we have sown) if we do not faint and give up. That seems easy enough, right? All we have to do is to stay focused, keep doing what we need to do and don't give in and before we know it we will have everything God has prepared for us. Well, it may sound easy to do, but everyone reading this book today knows it is not. We have an adversary who has been studying us all of our life and whose job is to steal, kill and destroy. This is why many of us shout over the promise but are tempted to give up during the process. We get discouraged, frustrated; we start to doubt and question whether we even heard God in the first place. I am writing my chapter to those who are starting to feel weary. I pray that the Lord will use my chapter and this book as a whole to strengthen, encourage and give you a second wind so that you can keep running until you run into all the Lord has already prepared for you.

Before becoming a Christian I lived my life in an unfulfilled way. I lived and did what I wanted but I did not feel happy or content. As a matter of fact, I felt depressed and empty. I always felt that I was called to do something, I just did not know what it was, and, as I result, I often tried to fill the void in different ways with many of those ways doing more harm than good. Even though I did not have a serious or deep spiritual connection I remember praying almost daily saying, "There has to be more to life than this!" That kind of prayer may have seemed strange and unnecessary to outsiders who looked at my life because on the outside I had a lot going for me. I was married, I was a nurse, I made good money, owned my own home, had good health and I was only in my late 20s. I had so much going for me and yet I felt depressed. Inside I was feeling like I should be doing something great in my life but I didn't know what it was and because of that I felt stuck, unproductive and depressed.

My life changed significantly when I became a Christian in 2003. I am not exaggerating when I say it felt like a light literally clicked on for me. All of a sudden my focus shifted from trying to figure things out on my own to dreaming and walking into purpose and blessings. Whether we know it or not we are all here for a purpose and until we tap into that purpose we will feel a void.

I think about the Children of Israel; in the book of Exodus they were slaves in Egypt for 400 years. During that time they cried out to the Lord for deliverance. This tells me that despite them being in bondage for a long time they felt there was more to life than their current situation. Even though there was nothing they could do in their own power and strength, they did not just accept living life and being in bondage. They cried out to the Lord daily and at the appointed time the Lord not only heard them but sent an answer. Look what Exodus 3:7-8[a] says: *The Lord said, "I have indeed seen the misery of my people in Egypt. I have heard them crying out because of their slave drivers, and I am concerned about their suffering. So I have come down to rescue them from the hand of the Egyptians and to bring them up out of that land into a good and spacious land, a land flowing with milk and honey."* (NIV) The Lord was speaking to Moses letting him know that He had seen His chosen people living in misery, He had heard their cries and that He was going to rescue them AND—don't miss this—He was going to bring them into a land that was good and spacious and flowing with milk and honey. The Children of Israel were not asking to have the additional blessing of land; they just wanted to be free. They had to know within themselves that they were called to be more than a slave, helping to build and establish someone else's kingdom. Little did they know the Lord already had a prepared place and prepared blessings for them; all they had to do was trust God and go through the process.

Hardly anything in life comes easy and if it does most of the time we do not appreciate it. Once the Lord through a series of miraculous events brought the Children of Israel out of Egypt the Bible tells us that the Lord did not take them on the shortest, easiest road because He knew that, if He did, when they faced war they would be tempted to turn around and go back into bondage. I believe the same is true for us today. The Lord knows the process each of us needs in order to strengthen us and make us ready for the manifestation of our dreams. It is not enough for our dreams to manifest; the Lord wants to make sure we know that it was He who allowed them to happen and He wants us to be able to maintain those blessings. *What good would it be for a man to gain the whole world and yet forfeit his soul?* Matthew 16:26 NIV. Our Heavenly Father knows just what we need to go through to be properly processed. The problem is, since we don't know, it can be scary and feel like it is too much to bear. Think about it; have you ever gone through a really tough time where you felt like you were going to lose your mind? Or it was so bad you wondered how you would ever make it though but somehow, some way you did and when you look back you see how you came out stronger with stronger faith? Most of the time, it is the hard situations and circumstances that help us to grow rather than the easier times.

I say this all the time, the Lord is raising up warriors and not wimps.

So how do you go through the process to bring forth your dreams without giving up?

1. Once you start moving toward your God-given dreams you have to know that it is not going to be easy. Sometimes the amount of warfare we experience is an indication that there is something great for us. The reason why the Children of Israel became slaves is because Pharaoh was able to see the great potential in them. Listen, the enemy often sees the greatness in us before we know it is there. You wonder why you have experienced childhood trauma and great warfare all of your life; could it be that the enemy was trying to take you out or mess you up so badly before you could ever walk in your purpose and calling?

2. Focus on what the Lord has done and what He is doing. As I mentioned earlier, the Lord brought the Children of Israel out through a series of miraculous events. They saw and experienced them firsthand and yet every time they came to another difficult period in their journey they forgot what the Lord had already done and they began murmuring and complaining. They started doubting if He was going to do what He said He would do. I can see why the Lord got frustrated with them! Imagine you made a commitment to do something for someone and you had already shown them you were a person of your word but they still continued to doubt you every chance they got. And not only did they doubt you but they became angry at you and talked badly

about you whenever things didn't go their way. Difficult times are our chance to show the Lord we believe Him no matter what! We can say we have faith all we want, but the only time faith is seen is when situations and circumstances are the exact opposite of what we are hoping for and yet we still have hope and believe. You may be thinking, *It's hard to believe God whenever things seem to be going wrong.* Here is what you need to remember: the Lord does not require us do what we are not equipped to do. He has given ALL of us a measure of faith and all we have to do is remember what He has already done in our life previously. He allows us to have experiences with His faithfulness in order for us to meditate on them while we are going through. The problem with the Children of Israel and many of us is that we rejoice when God moves in our life but then we get discouraged and give up during hard times. When David was getting ready to face Goliath, he remembered all of the previous victories the Lord had given him and was confident that the Lord would do the same with Goliath. "*The Lord who rescued me from the paw of the lion and the paw of the bear will rescue me from the hand of this Philistine.*" 1 Samuel 17:37 NIV.

3. Spend time in the presence of the Lord. This is essential to being able to fulfill your dreams. If your dreams are from God, well, it only makes sense that He will be the only one who can get you there. The ironic thing is that God gives us a dream and then we try to figure out how to get there on our own. It's like as soon as He speaks something we don't wait long enough to get the instructions or the blueprint. We hear part of the Word and then we are gone racing down the street,

going a way He never told us to go, and then we wonder why we get discouraged and frustrated. If it is a God-given dream it is going to take us working in conjunction with God in order for it to happen. This is why many times when God speaks something to us, if we are not careful we will reject it because it seems almost impossible for us to be able to do it. We don't have the right connections; we don't have the finances; we don't have the knowledge or skill set or it just seems like it can't be done by us.

Case in point: When the angel of the Lord told Mary she was going to have a son named Jesus, the first word out of her mouth was, "How?" She was asking how this could be since she was a virgin. Many of us say the same thing when God gives us a dream. We immediately look at ourselves and wonder how in the world it is going to happen. Well, the same response the angel of the Lord gave Mary he gives to us. *The angel answered, "The Holy Spirit will come on you, and the power of the Most High will overshadow you."* Luke 1:35 NIV. When the Holy Spirit comes upon us and overshadows us He anoints us and graces us to do what we are unable to do for ourselves. This is why we must stay in His presence. We do this by reading, meditating upon and living the Word, by praying at all times, especially when we feel weak and discouraged, and by worshiping and praising God. In the presence there is fullness of joy. He will speak to you and give you the encouragement you need to keep moving forward.

I remember when the Lord spoke to me over 11 years ago, telling me that I would publish books. At the time I had NO idea how in the world that would happen, but I believed God.

I prayed and when I felt compelled to do something I would do it. I registered my business; I opened up a bank account and did what I felt the Lord was leading me to do. I did what I could and before long the Lord sent people to do what I could not. The Lord connected me to people who each had a piece of the puzzle. I now have over 35 books published including Amazon bestsellers. To God be the glory! I share that to say you don't have to have all of the pieces right away. God will supply ALL of your needs when you need them. You do what you can do and trust God with what you can't do.

Finally, I want to say don't shout over the promise then give up in the process. We all get excited when we feel God has spoken a great promise or dream into our life, but we have to hold on when we are going through the process to prepare us for that promise. I love to surround myself with positive, inspirational things. In my office I have some wall posters; one of them says, "The pain you feel today will be the strength you feel tomorrow – Author unknown," and another one says, "Remember why you started. Don't give up; find another way – Author unknown." I want to encourage you to remember the joy and happiness when you first heard and believed in your dream. Hold on to that feeling and, when it starts to wane, ask the Lord to bring it back to your remembrance.

The Lord has placed great treasures and gifts within you in the form of dreams and visions; it is going through the process that allows them to come forth. It's not easy, but it is worth it!

Ayanna's Acknowledgments

I am thankful to the Lord for allowing me not only to publish this book but to serve as a co-author.

Thank you to the visionary of this project, Kishma A. George, aka the Purpose Pusher; that is truly who you are.

I am grateful for my family... My husband Blake, my daughters Shakiya and Lauriyana, my mother Margaret, sisters Sonya and Melody, my nieces, nephews and extended family.

My editor extraordinaire, Ken, thank you for your meticulous editing. You put the finishing touches on ChosenButterfly Publishing books.

Thank you to those who pray for me. You help me to keep pushing during the times when I feel like giving up...

Meet author Ayanna Lynnay

Ayanna's life is an example of how the Lord can transform a life and use that life to help transform other lives. After living a life of struggles and destructive behavior in early adulthood, Ayanna made the life-altering decision to surrender her will and accept the Lord's will for her life. It was then that the Lord began to reveal the purpose and plans He had for her life.

Wife- Ayanna is a wife, married to Blake Grantham, creator and editor of Unconfirmed Breaking News, a satirical website https://unconfirmedbreakingnews.com/ that you would have to be pretty crazy to read or just a little wacky… Blake is also creator of the game show *Opening Arguments.*

Mother- Ayanna is a mother to two beautiful daughters, Shakiya and Lauriyana, and numerous spiritual and godchildren.

Minister- She serves her local church, Tabernacle of Praise Buffalo, NY, under the leadership of Overseer Charles McCarley and Lady Rachel McCarley. Ayanna is the founder of The Transformation Station and S.O.S. Sisters of Strength Women's Fellowship, where women are healed, delivered, and strengthened so that they can help do the same for others. Ayanna loves to mentor and help birth women and youth into ministry. If you have ever heard Ayanna minister you will agree that she is real, relatable, transparent, easy to understand, powerful and yet humble. Sharing the message of hope and the power of God's transformation is the hallmark of how the Lord uses her.

Author and Publisher- Ayanna is also an author and founder of *ChosenButterfly Publishing* where books that transform lives are published. Ayanna has co-written four books dealing with the subjects of women in ministry, divorce, finding your purpose, living your dreams and more. Her first solo book project was titled *Devil, Please, I am Not Offended,* which deals with the relationship-destroying spirit of offense. ChosenButterfly Publishing has published over 35 books, some of which were Amazon #1 bestsellers in their category.

Ayanna wears many titles—wife, mother, nurse, author, book publisher, mentor, etc.—but the title that she takes most joy in is the title of transformed servant of the Lord. With a life dedicated to the Lord, Ayanna is transforming into the woman she never knew she could be and helping to transform other lives as well.

You can connect with Ayanna via social media

https://www.facebook.com/AyannaLynnay/

https://www.facebook.com/TheTransformationStation

https://www.instagram.com/chosenbutterfly/

Got a book you want to publish? Let's get it done

www.cbpublishing.com

Staying in His Presence

By Delsue Frankson

Developing a Relationship with God

The key to birthing the dreamer within and becoming all that God intended for you to be is to stay in the presence of God. In order to be in God's presence, you must first develop a personal relationship with Him. A relationship with God develops when we accept the Jesus as our Lord and Savior and we spend quality time meditating in His Word and communing with Him in prayer.

Proverbs 3:13–16 King James Version (KJV) says, "Happy is the man that findeth wisdom, and the man that getteth understanding. For the merchandise of it is better than the merchandise of silver, and the gain thereof than fine gold. She is more precious than rubies: and all the things thou canst desire are not to be compared unto her." See when we spend quality time with God, our wisdom will increase, and it will help us in all areas of our lives. Having wisdom will allow you to make decisions with confidence.

Proverbs 3: 26 (KJV) says, "For the LORD shall be thy confidence and shall keep thy foot from being taken." Walking in confidence will allow you to have opportunities that are not common to others. When your confidence is coming from God, your walk will be different, and your talk will be different. When you walk into a room, the presence of God will go before you and your presence cannot be ignored. God's presence will allow you to make the necessary connections needed to help you fulfill your dreams.

Proverbs 2: 6 (KJV) says, "For the LORD gives wisdom; from his mouth come knowledge and understanding." Having a relationship with God will equip you for your journey towards fulfilling your dreams. Therefore, let not your heart be troubled because God is in control. As believers the peace of God is with us and follows us wherever we go.

John 14: 1(KJV) reminds us to, "Let not your heart be troubled: ye believe in God, believe also in me." As we transition from childhood to adulthood, it can be a very scary and sometimes traumatizing experience at times, if no one prepared you for the adversities and the obstacles that you might face on your journey through life. Hiding God's Word in your heart will help you to safe and sound.

Psalm 91:4 (KJV) reminds us that "He shall cover thee with his feathers, and under his wings shalt thou trust: his truth shall be thy shield and buckler." I am encouraging you to continue to keep your eyes on Jesus. Put your trust and confidence in God and not man and watch how your life will change for the better overnight.

Jesus reminds us in John 14: 12–14(JJV), "Verily, verily, I say unto you, He that believeth on me, the works that I do shall he do also; and greater works than these shall he do; because I go unto my Father. And whatsoever ye shall ask in my name, that will I do, that the Father may be glorified in the Son. If ye shall ask any thing in my name, I will do it." What an amazing promise! This is what kept me focused on my journey through life.

Jesus also gave us another assurance in Matthew 28:20 (KJV). "Teaching them to observe all things whatsoever I have commanded you: and, lo, I am with you always, even unto the end of the world. Amen." I encourage you to work on your relationship daily with God; this is the foundation for achieving your personal goals and purpose in life.

Recognizing God's Voice

The ability to recognize God's voice comes from spending quality time with Him. A relationship with God will give you access to the Holy Spirit, who will lead and guide you in all conversations. The Holy Spirit will speak for you when you are unable to speak for yourself. The Holy Spirit will give you insight ahead of time so that you will be equipped and ready to face anything that you will be presented with. I am so grateful for this privilege that I have experienced so many times on my journey through life. God never leaves His children in the dark. I rejoice daily because God is my tour guide through life.

Psalm 16:11(KJV) says, "You make known to me the path of life; in your presence there is fullness of joy; at your right hand are pleasures forevermore." God wants what is best for His children. If we learn how to trust Him, He will give us better than we desire. God is the same yesterday, today, and forever. Just like how God spoke to the children of Israel and all the other prophets and leaders in the Bible, He continues to speak to us repeatedly through His Word today. It is so easy for us to forget who God is at times and that He sees and knows all. That is why it is important to stay in the Word. God has the solution to all of our problems. He instructs us in Jerimiah 33:3 (KJV) to "Call unto me, and I will answer thee, and shew thee great and mighty things, which thou knowest not." God always reveals what He is doing to His Children and provides guidance and provisions for the journey. But we must be intentional and ask Him for directions and continue to seek His face. Continue to put your faith and trust in God and allow Him to lead you and guide you on your journey through life.

Following God's Lead

It is not always easy to walk in obedience. We are gifted from our mother's womb. James 1:5 (KJV) says, "If any of you lack wisdom, let him ask of God, that giveth to all men liberally, and upbraideth not; and it shall be given him." Having wisdom will aid you in surrendering to the will of God. Success in life requires discipline. It is so easy to get distracted in life and before you know it, time has passed you by. There are so many different things around us that can easily distract us if we are not focused. We have to remember that everything in life is vanity, so don't get too obsessed with what everyone else around you is doing. Spend quiet time with the Lord so that you will be able to recognize His voice. Be very careful who allow into your personal space. Do not share your goals and dreams with everyone. It is so easy to abort your dreams and purpose because of the negative influence of others. Protect your peace and your space. Create a positive support system in your life. Surround yourself with individuals who will encourage you and also pray for your success in life.

We are all here for a specific purpose in life and our dreams and goals are usually tied to our purpose. Keep your eyes on the Lord and on your personal goals. There is sometimes a lot of organized chaos going on around us now, but we have to stay focused and not allow the chaos to bury what God has destined for you in life. There are a lot of people who you will see giving out directions on a daily basis. Every time you look around, you might see someone else who has a variety of suggestions. Seek the Lord before you make your decisions in life. He will lead you and guide you. Don't get discouraged by what is going on around you. Continue to look to the Word and God for guidance.

Staying the Course

It is so easy to give up, but you have to stay the course. There will be many distractions in life, but you have to stay focused if you want to achieve your dreams or fulfill your purpose in life. I want to encourage you to stay the course and pursue God's purpose for your life relentlessly. 1 Thessalonians 5:17 (KJV) encourages us to "Pray without Ceasing." Being relentless is a state of mind that can give you the strength to achieve, to survive, to overcome.

We have to remember that the Word tells us in Ecclesiastes 9:11 (KJV) that "I returned, and saw under the sun, that the race is not to the swift, nor the battle to the strong, neither yet bread to the wise, nor yet riches to men of understanding, nor yet favour to men of skill; but time and chance happeneth to them all." Our very existence is a reminder that God is not through with us yet. That's called purpose. You're alive for a reason, so don't give up. One of my favorite quotes is, "The task ahead of you is never greater than the strength within you (Unknown)."

I also love 1 John 4:4 (KJV), which says, "Ye are of God, little children, and have overcome them: because greater is he that is in you, than he that is in the world." Strive to be who God created you to be because you are irreplaceable. No one else can fulfill your divine purpose on Earth. Another one of my favorite quotes says, "What you do is important, but why you do it is more important. You must take intentional actions." (Bruce Van Horn)

We serve an intentional God. Circumstances should not determine our outlook on life, so we have to keep moving no matter what. As you continue to seek God's face on your journey through life, keep your eyes on Him. Some experiences will teach you a lesson and will only be for a season in your life. Sometimes you will be tested, but stay the course because you will gain wisdom from your experiences in life. James 1:2–4 (KJV) tells us, "My brethren, count it all joy when you fall into various trials, knowing that the testing of your faith produces patience. But let patience have *its* perfect work, that you may be perfect and complete, lacking nothing." I encourage you to continue to seek God's will for your life, so that you can learn the lessons He is teaching you or so that you can pass the test you are presented with on your journey through life.

The journey might get lonely at times, but God is with you, so don't lose faith and keep on moving forward no matter what. Take things one day at a time and one day you will start seeing the manifestation of the desires of your heart's desires. Whenever you come to a roadblock in life, reflect on the goodness of the Lord and don't forget where God has brought you from and what He has done for you in the past. If He did it for you before, He will do it for you again in the future.

Your vision might get blurry at times and in that moment when our way seems to get dark and you can't see the light at the end of the tunnel, just ask the Lord to help you. Joy always comes in the morning, my brothers and sisters. I just want to encourage you as you go about your day to continue to trust in God. Even though the road might get lonely sometimes, or you can't seem to find your way or balance in life, things will get better in time. Keep on moving forward because joy is coming in the morning. The God we serve usually brings about change unannounced. 2 Peter 3:8 (KJV) tells us "But do not forget this one thing, dear friends: With the Lord a day is like a thousand years, and a thousand years are like a day."

I just want to encourage you to be steadfast and unmovable as you work towards achieving your dreams or pursue your purpose. I know it is very difficult at times to be strong, but the burden becomes lighter when you turn it over to Jesus. God's Grace and Mercies are available to us morning by morning. Every day He gives us another chance to get it right and to draw closer to Him through the gift of salvation. As long as we stand firm in our faith, His mercies endure forever. 1 Corinthians 16:13, KJV encourages us to "Watch, stand fast in the faith, be brave, be strong." Life is not easy, but you can do it with the help of the Lord.

Ephesians 6:10, (KJV) reminds us "Finally, my brethren, be strong in the Lord, and in the power of his might." I will encourage you to be also mindful of the company that you keep and the choices you make on a daily basis.

1 Peter 5:8–9 (KJV) reminds us to "Be sober, be vigilant; because your adversary the devil, as a roaring lion, walketh about, seeking whom he may devour: Whom resist steadfast in the faith, knowing that the same afflictions are accomplished in your brethren that are in the world."

My brothers and sisters, there is nothing that we go through that is not already known to God. Don't lose faith because of what is going on around you, because God is in control and it is His will that will be done in your life and He will get the glory in the end.

My closing prayer for you is from Psalm 20:4–5 English Standard Version (ESV): "May he grant you your heart's desire and fulfill all your plans! May we shout for joy over your salvation, and in the name of our God set up our banners! May the Lord fulfill all your petitions!"

Delsue's Acknowledgements

I would like to dedicate my contribution to this book project to everyone who entered my life and made a positive difference. All glory, praise and honor belong to God for giving me the wisdom and knowledge needed to pursue my dreams and purpose successfully. I give God thanks for Dr. Kishma George for giving me the opportunity to share my personal experiences with birthing my dreams and fulfilling my purpose. Special thanks to my parents, Basil and Doreen Frankson, for being the best parents to a strong-willed little girl. Thank you both for supporting my dreams and for allowing me to spread my wings and fly. To my siblings and first friends, thank you for recognizing the calling on my life and for being my cheerleaders. To my amazing nieces and nephews, thank you for your continuous words of encouragement. Special thanks to all my so-called "Frankson Kids" who crossed my path as an educator. Thank you all for allowing me to make a difference in your lives, which helped me develop the skillsets that I have today. I pray that all will be blessed and will become successful in fulfilling their dreams and purpose in life. My goal in life is to encourage individuals to persevere regardless of the obstacles they will face in life. Walk in your destiny! Special thanks to all who supported the production of this book project.

Meet author Delsue Frankson

Delsue moved to the United States of America in 1987 at the age of 10 from Jamaica, West Indies with her family. She has resided in Florida for over 32 years. She is a minister at St. John Missionary Baptist Church in Boynton Beach, Florida under the leadership of the Reverend Dr. Jovan T. Davis, a life coach, consultant, artist, musician, designer, and model. She has been a professional educator for over 20 years and currently works as a behavioral health professional. She began her career as an assistant directress at West Glades Montessori in 2001 and became an Exceptional Student Education content equivalent math teacher in 2003. Since that time, she has had numerous professional opportunities and accomplishments in the areas of teaching, research, and service. She is a graduate of Florida Atlantic University where she received a Bachelor's Degree in Varying Exceptionalities in 2001 and a Master's Degree in Mental Retardation in 2003. She was the recipient of the I.M.P.A.C. Award for Individuals Making Personal Academic Achievements and giving back to their community from Florida Atlantic University in 2001. She was nominated twice by her colleagues for the prestigious Dwyer Award for outstanding educators in Palm Beach County. She was featured in the K.I.S.H. Magazine November 2019 issue and December 2019 issue as one of the Top 30 Most Influential Women: Movers & Shakers. She was also recently featured in K.I.S.H. Magazine spring edition in March 2021 as one of the Top 24 Trailblazers on the Move. She has participated in several university guest lectures at Florida International University on "Classification Issues & Placement Issues and Overrepresentation" of minorities in special education. She also presented at several professional national conferences on urban special education issues. She is a published author and the CEO of Delsue Frankson Consulting Services LLC. She recently launched her consulting firm's online training institute "Perseverance University" and a music therapy project for children, "Good Night." She is a model and fashion designer and her shoe brand "Grit" was recently featured in Italy, the United Kingdom, the United States of America, and Asia and in Elle magazine. She was initiated into the Xi Pi Omega Chapter of Alpha Kappa Alpha Sorority Incorporated in the fall of 2012 as a part of "The Ten Cultured Pearls." Since her initiation, she has served on the Xi Pi Omega Chapter's and The Alpha Pearl Foundation's executive committee boards. She participated in several service projects with the chapter and assisted the chapter in publishing their first history book. She is currently working on her Doctorate in Organizational Leadership, with an emphasis on k-12 leadership, at Grand Canyon University. Her desire is to complete her doctoral degree and continue to make a significant difference in the field of education, in her community and in the world. She brings her passion for service and for helping people to succeed and her experience as a leader and a team player to the field of education and the world. She hopes to continue to be an agent for change and to help others become productive and responsible global citizens.

Contact Information and Social Media Sites

Websites: www.delsuefrankson.com

www.perseveranceuniversity.com

https://grit.italianfashion.design

LinkedIn: Linkedin.com/in/DelsueFrankson

https://linktr.ee/DelsueFranksonConsulting

Facebook: Facebook.com/delsue.frankson

Facebook Business Page: @DelsueFranksonConsulting

Twitter: Twitter.com/DelsueFrankson

Instagram: Instagram.com/delsue_frankson

Email: delsuef@gmail.com

Phone: (954) 803-2722

My Breakup with Risk

By Dominisha Senegal

From time to time, we all will encounter a season of loss. I experienced many challenges in life and established a pattern of defeat before I even arrived at the start line. Delay equated to denial as I released doubt, fear, and insecurity. *How can I become excited about the **beautiful** promises I have yet to see?* was a thought that crossed my mind far too often. Church had become a cathedral of hit or miss. I read the Bible and didn't bother to remember the verses. I postured and engulfed myself in the distractions of the world; the broad way. I didn't want the narrow way. I ran; out of God's alignment, I ran. My doctrine became the songs, poems, and stories I wrote. The dreams that pawned my reality. The narrow way was too risky as I grounded myself on the world's principles and eventually wanted to give it all up.

In fact, one of the most liberating truths I have learned was I lacked.

I lacked a consistent prayer life, preparation and had no idea how to discover my purpose. Partly due to my disinterest, I misunderstood life and did not understand God at all. I had no clue how to even search for Him. Operating from a place of convenience, I began looking in all the wrong places, connecting to the wrong people; then, before long, I wound my way from the block to a New Jersey shelter.

Was God still able to use me? Well, sure, but not to the fullest capacity. Truth be told, I was too afraid to commit to Him. The scriptures say, "Commit thy way unto the Lord; trust also in him; and he shall bring it to pass." (Psalm 37:5, KJV)

"Bring what to pass?" I often questioned aloud, believing the audibly loud voice would grace me with the *deep, revelatory knowledge* I heard so much in church. Nope. I was wrong again.

Time progressed and so did confusion. Surviving an abusive marriage, my children and I entered into a domestic violence shelter.

I was brought to a place of brokenness, yet I wasn't ready to die; not to myself and certainly not without fulfilling my purpose. I didn't quite know how to. But one thing was for sure, I knew I had grown weary and felt God could not use me. Matthew 11:28 (KJV) says, "Come unto me, all ye that labour and are heavy laden, and I will give you rest." Amid life's distractions, I had to remain focused and figure it out. I needed a plan, and fast.

With my entire family back in California, I was left in such desolation. All I had was God, my children, and prayer. All I processed was indigence. In my possession were fragmented dreams. This was an unconcealable moment of the hidden truth, deeply spilling over into my misplaced faith and broken hymns. The battle between joy and shame presented a truth so strong I felt I'd die if I waited on God to move.

I found myself choked up with tears nightly. Dependency again became risky. It was in this very state that I felt scolded, empty, and ignored.

The heavy current facilitated the confessions that heisted my faith. I **prayed**.

I needed a refill; however, I recognized the fight, the deficit and financial *risk*. I then discovered this inner strength that did not belong to me. It was a goodness that I could not explain, but I wanted more. I was open to interpretation, though I did not want it. I began to invest in my connection with God. Conferences, seminars, and training. For so long I concealed the inner turmoil until it all combusted. I needed to see the God I knew I believed in; the God I had heard so much about—the One I searched for. My soul longed for the same God that performed the miracles and made the promises I reasoned to expect.

I **prayed**. Then, finally, I died.

One by one, they appeared—my answers. Risk and I were no more. We broke up. I continued praying, reconnecting to my source of strength, and the mustard seed of faith manifested. And so I continued investing. Some of the people who were around prior to my entry into the shelter began to ease out of the picture as I unknowingly took baby steps into alignment.

I shifted in a direction that began connecting me to the right people, who did not despise my small "new" beginnings. My faith did not collapse. Each person reengaged my spirit and taught me the strength within is deposited by the ultimate source—Jesus—which provides resilience and the ability to overcome. They were sent by God and they were answers to my many prayers.

I **planned**.

My circumstances were no longer taking the lead. Unbeknownst to me, my imperfections increased my faith. It was then that new approaches and possibilities never before established unfolded. I had an

Inheritance. It was my birthright; it was my purpose to start a transitional home for victims of domestic violence.

The blight experience was too great to cover up with a Band-Aid, but *healing* was just as painful. But, "He healeth the broken in heart, and bindeth up their wounds." Psalm 147:3 (KJV) became written upon my heart. It ushered an understanding of God's rewards. My fragile frame grew sturdy as I learned to fast. He rewarded my consistency of diligently seeking Him. I no longer consumed myself with the minutiae of what it appeared to be as Psalm 107:20 (KJV) turned into my new storyline: "He sent his word, and healed them, and delivered them from their destruction," and that is exactly what He did.

I began taking mini steps for what seemed like forever. However, this time, I did not stop. The momentum continued as I **prepared** my plan for **execution** of my newly found faith. I broke up with *risk* for good. There was no turning back; no more compromise. God continued to reveal Himself and I could not stop pressing forward. I discovered He works in cycles, so stopping was not an option; neither was giving up. And still, I prayed.

I began fleshing out my faith walk. Such simple words facilitated my serving and materialized expectation. The nucleus of the pivot caused a shift that could not be undone. My "small" start granted me access to the resources I otherwise would not have had by way of God's leading. I took one day at a time, asking God to show me the plans He had for me. Standing on the promise of Jeremiah 29:11, I fully surrendered and committed all that I am; a decision that formerly posed as a struggle. I connected to the plug of flawlessness—the Spirit of God.

My humility and experience began to work together for my good. With heightened awareness, I let go. Gratitude accompanied faith, which activated the currency of the assignment, to connect me with the manifestation of my inheritance—my purpose. I could not stop. For if I did, I could miss the open doors of opportunities again, causing a delay in the breakthrough. God continued to answer my prayers, and the inability to hear him properly could result in missteps and being placed in a holding pattern until He recycles back around. Diligence was key; to keep pressing toward the prize for the mark of the high calling, and it will surely come to pass.

"Being confident of this very thing that He which hath begun a good work in you will perform it until the day of Jesus Christ." Philippians 1:6 (KJV)

Dreaming was a privilege, though executing the prepared plan still required some level of faith. Insecurity attempted to arise as I did not feel qualified for the assignment. One afternoon, my spirit called out to The Most High God. It was a clear, subtle response. Just then, I was reminded of who my source is. My circumstances did not matter, nor did my shortcomings.

"If *it were something you can do yourself, then you would not need me,*" the voice resounded. "*I'm sending you help.*"

Interestingly enough, the perceived difficulty produced patience as I no longer focused on what was not happening. As difficult as it was, I kept my eyes fixed on Him. I had no other choice. He answered me and showed me great and mighty things. Through prayer I fought and through prayer I gained. There is no turning back. Looking to the Author and Finisher that saw the end from the beginning will never fail. Trusting in God is not an option, it is a privilege.

No matter the situation, we all experience a period of trial, test, and temptation. We can endure. Remember how far you've come. Stay focused and do not stop pressing forward. Each person has a destiny. And our destinies are connected to someone else's destiny. Recognize the toxicity, stumbling blocks, and distractions the enemy hurls to kill, steal, and destroy what God himself has placed on your life, your birthright—your purpose. Persevere through the "light" afflictions as you traverse on the journey of discovering your purpose and passion. Change will not always be a speedy process; however, the testimony will be far greater at the end.

Trust God's time and process. The inner realm of spiritual growth and power received will never coincide with the intellectual performance of the natural. A foundational prayer life is key and is essential to unlocking the questions and uncertainty of our mere existence. God is no respecter of persons. By keeping Him at the center of all that you do—tithing and sowing, worshiping, praising, and fasting—there is no doubt you will receive the much desired answer to your questions on this journey.

"But wilt thou know, O vain man, that faith without works is dead?" James 2:20 (KJV) Execution of your plan with prayer and faith is vital. Just as I heard that afternoon, that if it were something I could do myself then I would not need God, therefore it is not a Godly purpose. For if it is God who mandates the assignment, then He is obligated to provide the resources. You will not lose with God on your team. It is impossible.

The point at which we started does not matter. There is no speed race as it relates to fulfilling your assignment. Don't stop dreaming. Never stop moving. Never despise your small beginnings. Don't stop seeking God. He will perfect all that concerns you. The trials and tribulations will bring you to the revelatory place of pursuit. Never stop moving. Pray, create a plan, prepare it, then seek to execute the plan with faith—the currency of the given assignment that will connect you to the manifestation of the inheritance, which is your purpose. You deserve it.

Go forth with the confidence that God has a plan for your life. And He will never leave or forsake you.

Dominisha's Acknowledgements

I first want to acknowledge God the Father, Son and Holy Spirit, the true source of my inspiration. To HIM alone be all the glory as I am forever grateful for the preservation of life and the privilege to be HIS servant.

Earnest gratitude and appreciation to Dr. Kishma George and the Gleaming Dreamers family for giving me the opportunity and privilege of being part of an amazing movement. Thank you for all that you do and for selflessly extending yourself. I love you!

I want to express my love, appreciation and honor to my spiritual parents, leaders, mentors, and encouragers: Prophet/Senior Pastor Richard A. Gyamfi, Apostle Irene "Mamalistic" Gyamfi, Prophet Samuel O. Boakye, Prophet Okechukwu Nwachukwu and The Factory of God Church, Apostle Dr. Edison and Prophetess Dr. Mattie Nottage and Believers Faith Outreach Ministries, Int. Thank you for your leadership, mentoring, immeasurable support, encouragement, spiritual covering, rebukes, teachings and love. Endless love to Prophetess Deborah Santana, Pastor Linda F. Sauls, Minister Joy McIntosh, Bishop Claudia Ford, Pastor Oral and First Lady Angella Patrick, Apostle Dr. Gerald T. Hightower, Pastor Carrie Stroman, Prophetess Taya Algebra and the Stroman family, and Apostle Sharon Hamilton. I am forever grateful to The Most High for each of you. I love you all.

To my children: you are truly God's greatest gifts. Thank you for giving me a reason for it all. To my mother and entire family:

thank you for the continued support, love and encouragement.

Special thanks to Vickie and Phil Hamilton, Amanda Murray, Marc Chapman, GiGi, Alison Wilson, D. Botts, Marc Dorsey, Ana Ibacache, Brian Brown, and Barbara Shook Hazen. Thank you for believing in me.

segal Breakup Risk

Meet author Dominisha Senegal

As a believer of Christ, mother, author, writer, public speaker, songwriter and poet, Dominisha Senegal, also known as Domo, is no stranger to the community. She loves helping others and seeks to start a transitional living facility for victims of domestic violence.

Not only is Domo a writer and fireball, she is also an entrepreneur. Hailing from Los Angeles, California, she is also founder of THE B.L.O.C.Q., LLC. and THE WRITER'S BLOCQ, LLC., which strives to aid underserved and underprivileged young men and women to elevate and step into their purpose by way of the arts. She desires to leave a lasting legacy, not only for her children but one that will be a blessing to the community for generations to come; a legacy to empower and equip others with the ability to refocus and reacclimate themselves to creating a balanced and stable life of their dreams.

Honesty and Integrity come first in Dominisha's world. She began seriously writing while living in a domestic violence family shelter. Her works are deeply influenced by life's transactions and the hand she was dealt. Re-establishing herself on the scene, she began working at an accelerated pace. She collaborated with a multi-Platinum, Grammy-nominated music producer and singer/songwriter. Domo is set to release an EP in the near future.

You can reach Dominisha at:

DominishaSenegal@gmail.com and theblocq@gmail.com

Dominisha Senegal on Facebook and Instagram

Now Is The Time

By Rhasheeda Hague

God has something great for each of us to do while we are on this earth. He gives us beauty for ashes or makes something beautiful out of our mess. Jesus takes off our filthy garments and clothes us with a garment of righteousness. We must discover our purpose so our destinies can be fulfilled. When someone doesn't discover their destiny, they walk around empty, unsatisfied, and lost. However, when someone is walking in their destiny, they have a reason to get up in the morning, endure the storms, and keep going despite the hardships. We must trust the Lord so we can fulfill His plans for our lives. He will strengthen and guide you every step of the way.

Jeremiah 29:11 (ESV), "For I know the plans I have for you, declares the Lord, plans for welfare and not for evil, to give you a future and a hope."

Many people have regrets on their death beds because they ran out of time and never walked in their purpose. Time is something we can't get back. The clock keeps ticking regardless of who passes away. We must stop making up excuses. For instance, have you ever said, "I'm too old. I'm not smart enough. I'm not good enough. It's too hard. I will wait later"?

135

If anyone should make up an excuse not to walk in destiny, it should be me. I was molested multiple times as a toddler and it affected me in relationships and my viewpoint of God. Also, the enemy was playing with my mind saying such things as, "You will never make it. No one will ever love or care about you." I didn't realize that the enemy is a deceiver.

John 8:44 (NASB) says, "He was a murderer from the beginning, and does not stand in the truth because there is no truth in him. Whenever he speaks a lie, he speaks from his own nature, for he is a liar and the father of lies."

Since we know that the devil is a liar, why do we agree with his lies? The enemy does not want you to walk in your God-given purpose because he knows that lives will be saved, transformed, and empowered for Jesus Christ. It wasn't until I got a relationship with Jesus and experienced His love that I started on the journey to wholeness. Afterwards, the Lord sent several people in my life to encourage and mentor me. Through God, I was able to overcome and you can too. We are overcomers through Christ.

Romans 8:37 (NKJV) says, "Yet in all these things we are more than conquerors through Him who loved us."

I didn't let my past stop me and you should not either. Many people see the joy, prayers, prophecies, and the glory of God on my life. They see how my husband and I have a great relationship and our beautiful children. I didn't get here overnight. I had to go through a process.

We will go through trials and tribulations, but we must press past the adversity. Do you know what you are called to do? Where do you see yourself in the future? Are you walking in destiny? I have learned several key points when it comes to reaching for your future and fulfilling destiny: divine connections, accountability, knowing God's timing, serving, and prophecy. We will discuss each one.

DIVINE CONNECTIONS

When God gives you a vision, most of the time, it is bigger than you and you will need others to help you fulfill it. God will send the right people in your path to help and these key people are considered divine connections. I let God send them and I don't try to force a relationship that He never authorized. After we discern if they are from God, we gain a greater appreciation for their purpose in our lives.

I must give honor where honor is due. I didn't get to where I am today alone. God is so strategic because at different times, He sent people. The first divine connection is my husband. The other connections I consider them midwives because they helped to birth out the greatness within me. It's amazing how God used each of these individuals to take me to another level. I trust the godly counsel that each provides. Everyone needs a mentor, , or a spiritual parent because they have walked in places that you haven't or can give advice so you don't repeat the same mistakes they made. There are many mentors in the Bible. Jethro mentored Moses. Naomi mentored Ruth. Paul mentored Timothy. Jesus mentored his disciples. Elijah mentored Elisha. We all need someone. I will now share how these divine connections played a pivotal role in helping me walk in destiny.

My husband, Namun, loves me and has stood with me throughout the years. Without him, there would be no "The Day of the Daughters," which is the ministry God allowed me to be the visionary of. I am so blessed to be able to minister by his side in our ministry, "Wisdom for the Wilderness." Some husbands compete with their wives and are bothered by the anointing on them. Namun pushes me forward. He prays over me and speaks life into me. He encourages me and is my biggest supporter. God sent him into my life. Many women would love to do ministry with their husbands. God saw it fit when he partnered me with Namun. Long story short, we have to marry the right person. If not, then our destiny will be altered and we won't be able to do what the Lord is calling us to do. Pray before you say, "I do," and jump into something. You have to make sure that your union is God-ordained. Marriage is your first ministry and if your household is a mess, you won't have peace and will be less effective in your assignment.

Now, the first midwife I will mention is Apostle Desmon Dobbins. She is my spiritual mother, and I am an ordained prophetess through her school. God used her to build a foundation in my life. Everyone must make sure that the foundation is right because that is what you will build upon. The foundation is important to God and we must make sure that everything we do is built on Jesus, such as our marriages, relationships, businesses, etc., because it will last. Let's look at Matthew 7:24–27 (ESV).

[24] "Everyone then who hears these words of mine and does them will be like a wise man who built his house on the rock. [25] And the rain fell, and the floods came, and the winds blew

and beat on that house, but it did not fall, because it had been founded on the rock. [26] And everyone who hears these words of mine and does not do them will be like a foolish man who built his house on the sand. [27] And the rain fell, and the floods came, and the winds blew and beat against that house, and it fell, and great was the fall of it."

We need to be wise builders and build upon the proper foundation, so no matter what storm comes in life, we will make it with Jesus and His strength. A foolish person doesn't have the appropriate foundation.

I remember first going to Apostle Desmon's ministry. I was broken by some things in my past. I felt the love of God radiating from Apostle Desmon and other people in the ministry. I knew deep down that this was home for me. I submitted to her leadership, and God used her to instill fundamental truths from the Bible within me. I saw Apostle Desmon demonstrate God's love. I witnessed how God elevated her from prophet to apostle. The main thing Apostle Desmon taught me was how to have a relationship with Jesus and she always pointed me back to him. I was first introduced to the intimacy of the Lord, deliverance, and the prophetic through her. We need people in our lives who can introduce us to realms that we have yet to experience. In this walk, we must realize that Jesus is the source of our peace, strength, joy, protection, authority, breakthrough, and so much more. It's by His Spirit that we have help, counsel, and wisdom to get the blueprints and strategies to make it.

Next is Prophetess Kimberly Moses. Everyone calls her Prophetess K. Along this walk, we can get weary in our faith and go through wilderness seasons as we discover our purpose or go to the next level. I was dying spiritually because my gifts were not being cultivated and I found myself going through the motions in ministry. I was praying and crying out to God for help. I was yearning for more of God, and I knew there was more that I had yet to encounter. I needed to be poured into. Have you ever seen someone gasping for air? Well, that was me and the situation I was in. I was in a dry season and I was not growing spiritually.

After I cried out, the Lord then highlighted Prophetess K to me. He opened a door for me to connect and I took her training, "The School of the Prophets." The funny thing was that her school dealt with my character, which was a life-changer. Our character is everything and we need the characteristics of Jesus Christ, especially if we are His mouthpiece. Once a door opens, your character will keep you in the room. Her school really wasn't about prophesying even though we did that. Her training caused me to go deeper with God and boosted my confidence to prophesy. I became more confident in God and who He called me to be. I learned how to rely completely on God, especially with the prophetic exercises. Through the exercises there were so many words of knowledge spoken by her and others in the class. This class helped me to come back into alignment with what God was saying. The Lord used her to pour into me on another level and birth out some of the gifts within me. Prophetess K ministered to me, which caused intimacy with the Father to increase in my life. God breathed His life into me through her and my season went from dry to a level of abundance.

Everyone needs someone to invest in them and speak life into them. Some people are operating on fumes because they aren't spending time with God and don't have anyone to release the anointing into them. God used Prophetess Kimberly Moses to impart gifts in my life that only made me sharper for what I am destined to do. Impartation can take you to another level and bring you that much closer to reaching your goals. We can't be afraid to invest in our growth by taking classes, getting a mentor, or attending conferences. If we can spend major money on food, clothes, hair, accessories, or electronics, then why can't we invest in the Kingdom of God? Pray to God to attend a training and get mentors that will bring you a step closer to fulfilling your destiny.

The third midwife is Dr. Zolisha L. Ware. She would pray for me and prophesy to me on Prophetess K's prayer line. I can pick up the phone and call her about anything and she never judges me. Everyone needs someone in their life they can just be themselves with. If we have a bad day, we don't need people who will look at us like we are weak because we shed a few tears, got upset, or vented our frustrations. God places prayer warriors in our path to intercede for us because we will go through warfare. However, we aren't alone. When we feel weak, God will send people with His heart that we can trust to hold up our arms like Aaron and Hur did with Moses (Exodus 17:12). I have learned that you can't tell everyone everything. Believe God for trustworthy people in your life.

The next spiritual midwife is Dr. Kishma George, "The Purpose Pusher." I found her through Periscope, and I heard the Lord tell me that she would mentor me one day. Instantly,

I felt a connection and I learned many things from her. She has a motherly spirit and she always pushes me. At the right timing, the Lord connected us. Before then, I would watch her broadcasts and the gifts on the inside of me would be stirred. She made my baby leap every time I listened to her minister. God was using her to pour life into me. It's amazing how everything just built up. It was almost like I was pregnant and going through different trimesters. I could literally feel all the birthing pains.

Luke 1:41 (NLT) says, "At the sound of Mary's greeting, Elizabeth's child leaped within her, and Elizabeth was filled with the Holy Spirit."

We need people who will stir us up so we don't get comfortable. If we stay in our comfort zone, we will never get the full harvest that God has for us. I remember the day when God told me, "Now is the time for you to connect with her." When He gave me the green light, everything fell into place. I called Dr. Kisma George and the Lord used her to birth great gifts out of me and accelerated me to my purpose.

Lastly, the Lord connected me to Prophetess Nicole. I meet her through Dr. Kishma George's broadcasts. God used Prophetess Nicole to deliver me from some childhood issues when God said, "Now is the time for it to come to the forefront."

When I was molested as a toddler, the enemy tried to make me feel like I was crazy. He would say, "No that didn't happen." It did occur and God used Prophetess Nicole to get to the root of the issue and cast it out. If we want to be used by God in a greater capacity, we must get delivered from the strongholds that can hinder us in our future. I refused to allow the enemy to have anything over my head. My Lord and Savior Jesus Christ died on the cross for my freedom. Apostle Paul said that he continued to press forward and we must do the same.

Philippians 3:14 says, "I press toward the mark for the prize of the high calling of God in Christ Jesus."

ACCOUNTABILITY

The next key point in Reaching For Your Future And Fulfilling Your Destiny is Accountability. Many have died prematurely or are no longer operating in ministry because they had no one to keep them in check, tell them no, or correct them when they were wrong. Each of the individuals above are my accountability partners. I check in with them for various reasons and it has helped me to stay on the straight and narrow path with Jesus Christ. I told the Lord that I don't want to do things just to be doing them. I purposely make sure that God is in everything I do and my accountability partners are spirit-filled. You must make sure that there is someone on this journey who will hold you accountable because there is so much at stake. It's not just about you but your family, future, business, ministry, souls, etc. If you want longevity and don't want to be a one-hit wonder in the spirit, find someone to hold you accountable. We need someone who can look past our gifts and talents to deal with us.

Zachery Tims, a well-known evangelist, died from a drug overdose. He was cheating on his wife and he didn't have many people to hold him accountable. After he fell away from God, he was sat down for three months. However, they knew he could preach and draw a big crowd, so they released him again to do ministry prematurely, which resulted in his demise. Joyce Meyer was sat down for three years by her leadership, which allowed her character to be developed in Christ. As a result of her submission, God blessed her with longevity and a worldwide ministry. William Braham was a powerful prophet, but he erred because he wanted to be a teacher. God didn't call him to be in the office of a teacher. He started teaching false doctrine and he only had "yes" men around him or those who only told him what he wanted to hear. William got rid of anyone who went against him or tried to warn him of his erroneous ways. He tragically died in a car wreck. Had he listened, he might have lived longer because when you are in the will of God, you will be safe. A real accountability partner will tell you the truth even if it hurts. It's better to be corrected so the mistakes can be dealt with and you can be pleasing in the Lord's sight.

KNOWING GOD'S TIMING

Many people don't discern the Lord's timing. They are frustrated because they thought something was going to happen overnight. Just because you receive a prophecy doesn't mean it's going to happen right now.

2 Peter 3:8 (NKJV) says, "But, beloved, do not forget this one thing, that with the Lord one day *is* as a thousand years, and a thousand years as one day."

One day with the Lord is as a thousand years! Imagine now receiving a prophecy that says soon or now. It may not be as soon as you hoped. However, that doesn't mean that God won't fulfill

His promise. We just have to wait or be patient, which is one of the fruits of the Holy Spirit (Galatians 5:22–23).

I learned how to discern God's timing by having His peace about something. For instance, I will pray and ask, "Lord, is this something You want me to do?" If I feel uneasiness, then His answer is no. However, if I feel His peace, then it's yes. I will still have God's peace throughout the obstacles. Sometimes, I hear the voice of God, directing and preparing me for the next step. Are you feeling God's peace about a certain person or situation? If not, take heed because you need to make sure you are aligned with Him. The enemy would love to derail your destiny and cause you to be misaligned.

I also discern God's timing by the open door. God will open doors that no one can shut (Revelation 3:7). He longs to bless us but we must know which doors He opened for us to walk through. For instance, when a door opens, I pray and if I have the Lord's peace, then I know I can access it. God has opened doors for me to minister on many platforms. Most of the time, I didn't ask Him for it. He had already prepared me to walk in purpose because I spent time with Him. Don't neglect time in the Word because it's sharpening you to do great exploits for the Lord. We don't have time to go backwards because we have so much work to do for the Kingdom of heaven. If you are submitted to God, then He will not allow you to walk through demonic doors.

We must pray, fast, and be obedient to God so we can build our relationship with Him and align ourselves with His timing. When we are in the presence of God, He will speak to us. His sheep know His voice, which will get rid of any doubt or confusion.

When I spend time with God, I receive clarity and I no longer question Him about my purpose.

John 10:27 says, "My sheep hear my voice, and I know them, and they follow me."

We don't have to make things happen or get anxious about them. We don't have to conjure up things. God will establish everything in His time. He created us and formed us before He formed us in our mother's womb. We need to rest in Him. God told me that we need to enjoy the journey. Often we miss out on so many things because we are so focused on the promise. God did so many miracles for the Israelites while they were in the wilderness. We must trust and enjoy the process and not rush it. The process and wilderness are necessary.

Imagine an obituary. There is a dash between the year that a person was born and their death date. That dash represents the journey. There were so many things that the person experienced, good and bad. If we would just learn to change our perspective and realize that all things are working together for our good, then we will learn how to enjoy the process. Then we will start to look at the hardship (wilderness) differently.

SERVING

What you make happen for others God will make happen for you. For years, I have been so busy serving others, helping them with their vision and walk into their destiny. Miraculously, one day, the Lord started doing it for me. He told me, "You have been faithful, Now Is The Time!" He sent so many confirmations saying the same thing.

Luke 16:12 (NKJV) says, "And if you have not been faithful in what is another man's, who will give you what is your own?"

For instance, I don't mind sharing or promoting someone else's ministry because I know that one ministry doesn't have everything and I want people to get the resources they need. You never know what someone is going through. I always want to share Godly content because it could be the answers to someone's prayer.

Since I have sown support into others, I reap support. I have embraced myself as a distribution center and God uses me to connect others. We must understand that we are the body of Christ and we are composed of many members. When we have a revelation of that, we don't try to hold things or keep people to ourselves. The body takes every part to be complete. If you have a part that will help someone, then I want you to share it with others.

For years, I was Apostle Desmon's armor bearer and I learned humility. Humility will take us far in life. Elisha served Elijah for many years before he even started his own ministry. As a result, he received the double portion. The double portion came through a relationship and was a double portion of Elijah's spirit. In other words, because Elisha served Elijah, he received his inheritance and was able to do twice as many miracles as his leader.

PROPHECY

God has spoken to me through several other vessels as well. Prophet Oliver and Prophetess Annette Keanon are two prophets who gave me specific words about my purpose. Prophet Oliver gave me a detailed word about God's timing and angels. Then, one day, I went to a conference that the Lord told me to go to. God used Prophetess Annette to speak the month when God would reveal my purpose. God is so specific.

Recently, the Lord has given me the green light and said, "This is the season."

From August to September 2020, a supernatural thrust took place. Things started to take off. I was like, "Whoa! Is this really happening? All of the words, dreams, and visions have started coming to pass or into fruition." I am so in awe of God and many times I have to get my mind together. God reminded me of how faithful I have been.

For years, there were many promises spoken over my life. Now I am seeing manifestations. Once I received instructions from God and confirmation from others, I began to take another step on my journey. Do you have divine instructions? How do you know that you are doing what God authorized for your life? Once we hear from God, there can be no doubt or fear. We know that we have the Lord leading and guiding us every step of the way. God has spoken things to me that I thought I could never do. That is the power of prophecy. It births something greater on the inside and we begin to change our perspective. We start to think bigger and want what the Lord wants. Don't despise prophecy because God has something great in store.

Meet author Rhasheeda Hague

Rhasheeda is a wife, mother of four, prophetic intercessor, mentor, teacher, and entrepreneur. Rhasheeda was ordained as a prophet in October 2020 by her spiritual mother, Apostle Desmon Dobbins, through Kingdom Principles Learning Centa. Her relationship with God is the most influential aspect of her life. Rhasheeda is consistent in her work ethic, a trustworthy, dependable, responsible, and loving individual whose life can be defined by the way she loves. She enjoys serving others.

Rhasheeda and her husband founded "Wisdom for the Wilderness," a ministry that grants individuals the spiritual, mental, emotional, financial, and social support they need to grow and be successful. Rhasheeda is the visionary of "The Day of the Daughters," a nonprofit that focuses on building daughters of all ages through offering services and resources that encourage wholeness in spirit, soul, and body.

Rhasheeda is the host of "Daughters Talk," a weekly Facebook and YouTube Live that addresses and discusses important matters that daughters go through and offers them tools to change their situation. Rhasheeda is also the visionary of "Daughters Spotlight," which spotlights women of influence monthly. She also hosts "Wednesday Night Live Prayer" on Facebook and Instagram.

The Dreamer In You

By Chuntae Nicole

~ Finally ~

I never thought in a million years that I would be living my dreams. But here I stand out of the rubble and the fog full of courage, faith, love and passion. If you knew my start, my story of how life just happened at the age of eight years old—the sexual abuse, the abandonment and the rejection—I should have not only given up, but I should have lost my mind ... yet I stand. Dreams no longer delayed and hope no longer deferred, this simple Southern girl with big dreams who was knocked off her feet and derailed for 30 years made it. My "it" may not be your "it", but it's mine.

I was the little girl who lived in a bubble, too withdrawn and too guarded to really engage or live for real. Who was I anyway? No affirmations and no words of encouragement, seen and not heard, I was lost. I was waking up every day going through the motions of life, too uncertain about who I was and too afraid to fail to live. But this girl got her life back. This girl, this dreamer, now knows what it means to go from feeling like no one and nothing to becoming this lion that FINALLY got her roar.

Dreams always seemed to be so far-fetched growing up. I guess because I never saw anyone that I knew live their dream. The idea of dreaming seemed like it was for the super special people, not the ordinary person I thought myself to be. In my world, dreams were just that ... a dream. They were something in your head that you thought about and imagined so grand, or a place to escape to... That was the extent of what I knew a dream to be; that is until ... I discovered me.

I discovered that I was not a nobody walking around in this world; that just because I had scars, just because I had bruises, it didn't mean I was worthless. I discovered I was powerful beyond measure. I was not my pain, my trauma, my abuse or my past. I was the very image of my Father. I discovered that I was accepted before the foundation of the world was created; I had My Father's DNA running through my veins; I WAS one of those super special people, and so are you! My life changed when I learned my name. When I accepted what my Father said about me— that I was chosen, that I was wanted, that I was His beloved—I discovered me. Yes, I FINALLY understood that if my Father was great, so was I. If He could create, then so could I. If He was powerful, then so was I. If He could flatten mountains and walk on water, then so could I!

I FINALLY understood who I was when I really stopped to look at Him. Looking at my Father caused me to see me. All those 30 years of fumbling around in the dark searching for where I belonged, where I fit, asking others where was my place in this world; I found myself still searching. I looked to everybody else for my identity, when none of them were fit to tell me... Eventually

I came to the end of myself, full of despair, emotionally fatigued, spiritually destitute and barely breathing; and it was at this point in my life that my Father began to speak to me. He said to me that no matter how long I wanted Him to hold me He would. He told me that He never got tired of listening to me. He said that I was His favorite, and there I lay in my Father's arms.

There was something about knowing that I am loved that fueled me to dream. Just knowing that my heavenly Father loved me and approved of me made me feel good about myself. I had no idea how much the right approval could change me forever. This was the missing piece that I needed to catapult me from barely breathing to dreaming... God's approval is the stuff that dreams are made of... He told me that He had a plan for me, and this time I believed it. This time I knew Him for real. I knew of Him before from family and people at church telling me about Him, but when He showed up to rescue me from the doorway of a mental institution, when I believed my only peace was my lifeless body lying at the bottom of a bathtub full of water, I knew the God of the Bible was real to me ... and He loved me. This is a fact that I am now most certain of. This is what every dreamer should have in their back pocket. When you feel like you have nothing else to give, when you become unsure of your next move or you find yourself running low on strength, this is what you need to remember. God is rooting for you from the heavens.

So, I met God, and He began to speak to me, and He healed my broken heart, and He delivered me from those 30 years of rejection and abandonment and torment from abuse. He taught me how to forgive, how to trust and how to love again. It wasn't until my trembling heart was healed that I felt free to dream the real dreams that I always had from childhood. But it didn't start out like that. It started out with a frail little "Yes." That's all I had. I was like an abused little animal that was left out in the street to fend for itself when I began to dream again. If someone tried to help me my guards would go up instantly, so it wasn't overnight. It was a process of saying, "Yes." God did not crack the sky and come down from heaven to help me, my help came in the form of people; destiny helpers. These destiny helpers were equipped to handle me in my frail state, and I knew that it was God because He let them see me for who I was becoming. He gave them a heart for me. God had spoken to them about me, and He had spoken to me about them. God knows where each of us are and who and what we need for our next.

My little yes unleashed the greater in me. I didn't know at that time that what was locked up inside of me was greatness, but it was. Never would I have imagined that I had multiple books inside of me. I didn't know that there were curriculums, ministries, conferences, and businesses in me. And the astonishing thing about it all is that we don't have to know. All it takes is a "yes" to the One who does know. See, we didn't make ourselves, so we can very well live our lives not knowing what we are truly capable of accomplishing. This is why our "yes" is so crucial. What I mean is by saying "yes" to God we are choosing to cooperate with the plan of God for our lives in order for Him to perfect the plan that He intended for our lives. Our destiny and purpose is great because He is great, and He is the only One who knows us fully. When we go back to Him to get the instructions, the blueprint and the insight, we then can birth what's in us. He put all the gifts, skills, abilities and talents inside of us, so it's going to take us partnering with God to bring it out of us.

What is your dream? What is that thing you see yourself doing that's bigger than you? Everyone has something that they see themselves doing or having that seems too big to accomplish on their own. I really want you to think about these questions honestly. When you truly answer these questions, there will be something in your mind's eye that seems a little silly to believe is possible, but at the same time it is exciting yet frightening to tackle. This is the stuff that dreams are made of. The dreams that God gives us are supposed to be too big for us to accomplish on our own. They're too big for us to do on our own because God intended for us to partner with Him to accomplish them. The wonderful thing about partnering with God is that you don't have to know what you're doing; it may seem foolish to say, but it's true. Again, all that matters is that God knows what He's doing. All you need to do is to see the dream and have faith in God as He tells you what to do. He may not take you directly to the dream head-on; He may take you to the dream through an unconventional way! I personally stumbled into my purpose. I had no clue that me writing a book would open the door for innumerable opportunities, magazines, TV and radio show interviews, businesses and national and international speaking engagements.

You see I stumbled to the doorway of my dream at a time when I felt helpless. I was suicidal and filled with despair, and God sent a destiny helper to pray me out of that place. God began to breathe for me when I needed spiritual resuscitation. You may be experiencing pain so excruciating that it paralyzes your ability to think clearly, and you may feel like you have to get yourself together in order to live your dream, but I am living proof that you don't. All you have to do is believe God. God sent someone with a Word from Him when I was losing my mind, and I began to grab hold of that Word and live. See sometimes you may not even have strength for yourself, that's okay. Do you have faith? That's enough! Grab hold of whatever God says, and DO IT. That's what I did. When you have nothing else to lose, you have everything to gain. God told me to write. He told me to spill the pain out on the pages. I had so much pain that I just wanted to die and here was God telling me to write until I felt relief. So, I did. This is how my first book, *How I Survived*, was written. Little did I know that this was the beginning of me birthing my dreams. This book filled with so much transparency became a tool to set millions of people free.

As I wrote God healed me, page by page, chapter by chapter; this book was a prophetic key to the door of my freedom spiritually, mentally, emotionally, and financially. This is why we have to partner with God. Understand that it wasn't the book that changed my life, it was my obedience to God that changed my life. I didn't know that this one simple act of obedience that I did by faith at the worst time of my life would change my life forever.

It's our obedience to God, nothing else. God could have told me to make a kite and my obedience would still have caused me to birth my dreams. What is it that God is telling you to do that seems too big, too scary, too foolish to do? DO IT ANYWAY! This is your place of change. This is your place of turnaround.

Oftentimes, what weighs heavily on our minds are the precedents of man; the logic of man or "the way that things are supposed to be done" that hinders our faith in what God says. But this is why we have to stop rationalizing away what God has spoken. As you read this, you will be reminded of things that God has been speaking to you that you have yet to move on because you don't have it all figured out. I dare you to just do what God has told you to do and let God worry about the outcome. This is how you move from the realm of just dreaming to birthing your dream.

There are many that will tell you what you risk losing if you do that thing that God has been speaking to you. Fear will creep in and try to discourage you and even remind you of your past failures and what you lost. But the truth is when I said, "Yes," to God, the truth is I did lose a lot. I lost my despair; I lost hopelessness and complacency; I lost a monotonous nine-to-five career; I lost a lack of faith in my God; I lost rejection. My "Yes" was a seed and what I have gained from that "Yes" I am still reaping. In exchange for my despair and hopelessness He gave me courage and set my life on fire. In exchange for my monotonous nine-to-five God gave me businesses and made me my own boss. In exchange for my lack of faith God pulled me in closer and showed me how to live by the words that He speaks to me daily. In exchange for my rejection, He made me a carrier of His glory and showed me how to live in His presence.

It does not matter what everyone else around you may say or may think, all that matters is what God says and what you choose to believe. As I did what God told me to do, He surrounded me around other dreamers. There is another realm in which dreamers live. Dreamers are willing to move when God speaks without having to have everything nailed down. I did not understand this initially, but as I moved at God's words to me, my life as I knew it changed and I found myself in the company of dreamers. My mind changed as I continued to extend my faith and just moved when God said, "Move." As God said, "Write," I wrote. As He said, "Go," I went. As God said, "Speak," I spoke. This is the atmosphere of the dreamer, and this is how you give birth to your dreams. This is how to move past fear, doubt and unbelief. How can you birth your dream if you are surrounded by these things? Mindsets are atmospheric. The mind can be impregnated with doubt or it can be impregnated with faith, and those around you may or may not intentionally cast doubt or fear on you, but birthing should occur in a place or atmosphere where it is safe to deliver.

God wants to birth the dreams that He placed inside of you. He can handle the birthing if you can see it and believe Him. He can handle the rest. He doesn't need your help; He just needs your cooperation. It took me losing everything before I finally cooperated with God, but that does not have to be you. Today can be the day that you abandon your fear of failing or not knowing what's next and just do what God has shown you or said to you. When you think what you're doing is not going to be enough is the time when God steps in and gives you the next piece, and the next piece and the next. And when you find yourself at this place, know that you have shifted into the realm where dreams are birthed.

Prophetic Decree

I decree that you are entering into the realm of the dreamer; that you are shifting from the place of stagnation and complacency. Your eyes will see your dreams coming to fruition, and your garments and your speech will match your dreams. The pieces to the puzzle of your life will form the master plan that God has for you. You will not be bound by fear, but you will leap like a gazelle into destiny and purpose.

Chuntae Nicole's Dedication & Acknowledgements

I dedicate this book to all of those who think dreaming is for the extra special. Know that you are one of the very special ones, and the world is waiting to meet you!

Special thanks to:

My first midwife, Prophetess Adonn'ah Morris, The Master's Mouthpiece. God used you to walk me through the toughest time in my life and I am eternally grateful. Love is an action, and you not only exemplify that, but your life demonstrates it to me. I love you.

Overseers Apostle Byron H. Lampkin & Pastor Patricia Lampkin, Word of Faith Outreach & Deliverance Ministry. Thank you for praying with me and covering me and seeing who I was and pushing me forward to do what God has called me to do. Thank you for not clipping my wings. You took me in when others rejected me. How can I ever say thank you enough?

Dr. Kishma George, Birthing the Dreamer in You Mentorship Program, you showed me how to get this book published. You walked me step by step through the process and invited me onto platforms for which you had already paved the way.

Prophetess Cherieka Spells, Internationally Cherieka Spells Ministry. God only knows how you helped me become one with my voice, my sound, with me! There is no price to pay to have my voice back. Thank you!

Thank you to my daughter, who patiently let me take the time I needed to heal.

Thank you to my small but mighty circle of prayer warrior sisters who pray me through each project and assignment that God has given me. Each of your faces flashes in front of me right now. I love you all!

Meet author Chuntae Nicole

Chuntae Nicole was born in 1982 in West Palm Beach, Florida. She is the third of four children born in the marriage between her mother and father. She also has other siblings whom she loves and adores. She is known for standing for what is right, no matter the consequences. Chuntae Nicole is serious about her conviction to God and loves justice and equality. Her family moved around a lot, but finally settled in her later childhood years in Philadelphia, Pennsylvania when she was 14 years old. She served in her family's ministry as an executive secretary, treasurer, Sunday school teacher, president of youth department, worship leader, tutor and director of dance ministry before and after she went away to college.

Chuntae Nicole graduated from Pennsylvania State University in 2005 with a Bachelor of Arts degree in Labor and Industrial Relations and a minor in African and African American Studies. She endeavored to use her skills to level the playing field in the labor industry and ensure that employees not only knew their rights but could identify when they fell prey to unfair labor practices in the workplace. Two of her greatest joys are song and dance, and while in college she performed with the West African performing arts company Nommo and performed in song for Essence of Joy Ensemble.

Chuntae Nicole served eight years in the military and was discharged honorably as a staff sergeant in 2009. In 2008, she gave birth to her daughter, Elizabeth, and shortly afterwards began working for a non-profit drug and alcohol treatment organization as a risk manager, internal auditor, safety manager and instructor. After many years at the organization, she left corporate America and partnered with a full-service financial firm. Throughout her life, Chuntae Nicole has displayed a heart to mentor and encourage individuals to see their God-given potential and enable them to leave this earth, as Miles Monroe would say, "empty." She recently launched her women's ministry, "Mary's Ministry International," and uses this platform to bring inner healing, support and encouragement to all women who need help and want healthy insight into various issues that plague the hearts of women across the world. She is the author of *How I Survived; The Key to Being Set Free* and founder and CEO of Pure Hearts Ignited, Inc.

She is an inspirational speaker, entrepreneur, mother, advocate of justice and equality and woman of God who is willing to leave the 99 for that one who may have gone astray. Anyone who knows her will concur that she is known for speaking up and speaking her mind, although over the years she has learned that a still tongue makes a wise head. Now Chuntae Nicole listens and waits on the leading of the Holy Spirit for direction and continues learning from the One who is a perfect teacher who leads her and guides her into all truth, her Heavenly Father God.

Prophetess Chuntae Nicole serves under the oversight of Apostle Byron H. and Pastor Patricia Lampkin of Word of Faith Outreach and Deliverance Ministries, Inc. in Darby, PA.

The Manifested Promise

By Ronisha Williams

Has your faith ever been shipwrecked? Has your life ever been wrecked by a storm you didn't see coming? Have you ever been faced with a life crisis and broken relationships? I remember being paralyzed and the doctors giving up on me, yet God brought me through it. I remember being intubated 58 times and each time God brought me through it. I remember overcoming molestation, insecurities, rejection and abandonment; God did it. I remember being left, misunderstood, not having true relationships in my life because of my past hurts, letdowns and failures and abuse, but God.

This last test shifted the very course of my life and realigned me for purpose. I never thought my life would be shaken the way it was, but looking at it now, it was all a part of God's master plan. Have you ever had a storm catch you off guard? That was me. I never saw me losing my baby, all I saw was everything working out. To be honest, looking back I was so caught up in the process that I missed all the signs. When it happened, it hit like a ton of bricks, my whole life shattered. It felt as if my heart was ripped right out of me. For weeks after losing my baby I wept, I screamed and I hollered. I could not wrap my mind around the pain, it was

165

so deep.

In the midst of me going through this every relationship in my life began to fall off. I went through blow after blow and I couldn't understand why. I didn't even have the strength to even find out why at the time. I experienced accusations of stuff I wasn't even close to ever doing, but I had to go through it. God spoke to me and said this was all for His Glory. At the time I was like, *How God? I'm shattered; I'm broken; you took the very thing that was a promise from me.* All this was going on, yet God had a master plan already working together for my good.

I was fighting through a deep pain that even I could not articulate. I was pushed and people kept telling me, "It's God's will, you can have another one." Yes, all that is true, but that religious spirit is distasteful. That was insensitive and it was not what I needed, I had just lost my baby. My heart was so fragile and people kept saying, "You're so strong." I actually wasn't; that was a weak moment. Even the strongest people become weak and it's imperative you are around people who can carry you. I didn't need judgment; I didn't need to be misunderstood. I needed love and compassion. Even in the midst of one of the greatest shifts in my life it was some of the deepest pain. I cried and I cried to God; I was finally truly broken before Him. I was empty so that He could fill me back up again. With this next fill-in God was about to thrust me into overflow. As I cried in my prayer closet He took me to Job 3:25. "For the thing which I greatly feared is come upon me, and that which I was afraid of is come unto me."

God dealt with me about fear and how the very thing Job was afraid of came to him. This was me; I was afraid of failed relationships, miscarrying, and submitting to leaders because of past spiritual abuse. I was flowing in ministry bound by fear and didn't know it.

Once God revealed it to me, He walked me through deliverance and fear was dismantled. I promise you at that very moment my eyes were immediately open. There was something on the inside of me that shifted. I can't even articulate how God began to move afterwards; it was just that powerful. What I was blinded by was no longer there and God began to move mightily. God started to speak strategically to me about this next move in my life. After a year of knowing who my leaders were I was able to obey Him. I submitted to my leaders and from that day my life shifted in a notable way. I mean it began to take off without fear, without reserve. And for a particular situation in my family we were finally beginning to see justice. Relationships that I knew I should have fought for were restored; friendships that I had for years were reconciled. Then God started to shift the totality of my entire life.

As I began to execute in ministry, miracles started happening and became frequent. My finances catapulted to another realm, I can't even explain it the way God is shifting. My entire life has changed, God wiped out my life to realign me all for His glory. It took losing something so precious to me (my baby), yet I gained something much greater. Now I also am carrying my next baby to full term. The last five years of my life were a complete whirlwind with test after test. It was hard being without a church family and not having a leader, but God knew I wasn't ready and this was divine timing. I was pushing in ministry but deep inside I knew God had to take me through again to truly get me to where He wanted me. At this point in my life all that matters to me is what matters to God. I must embody Him in this hour in order to manifest Him the way His Word declares.

As God began to shift my life He started to send authentic voices such as my leaders to speak a word. It was something I knew only me and God knew. I knew from the time I was a little girl I was cut from a different cloth. I could never fit in and honestly I really don't want to. I want God for real. I was at a place in my life where I was tired of being sick and tired. I desired to see a real move of God. I was tired of seeing people bound and staying bound, broken and not free. God knew exactly how to get freedom to me first so that I could execute His agenda in the kingdom. As God began to restore and move, His ministry within me started to take off on a whole new scale. God began to pour out the mysteries of his Word in a way I hadn't experienced in my life. As I began to move in the obedience of God every time I trained a Bootcamp class God began to outpour miracles. He healed a baby right on my FB live. God healed a woman with scoliosis right in my training. Pain, diseases, and sickness went immediately. I was a miracle to manifest miracles. God is truly living out His God-sized dream within me. Destiny caught me.

So often we pray and want God but don't want the sacrifice that comes with it. Or we want God and just don't know how to activate Him in our life. We are in a time where we must truly have God for real. Your dreams, destiny, and purpose mean nothing outside of God. We need to embody Him in everything we do. What does it mean to embody God? It means to inherit who He is and demonstrate it with power and authority. "Em" means to put in, so we are putting all of who Christ is on the inside so that He can exude out of us.

I shared all this to let you know you can make it through anything with God being the forerunner of your life. It may look dark and dim, but trust God. Your dreams and purpose are aligning with the will of God for your life. Keep pushing because on the other side is joy unspeakable. It's an intimacy with God that's so saturating. God is putting His fire behind His voices in this hour. Let your process birth the fire of God so it can exude out of you as you walk out your God-given dreams and destiny. Romans 8:28 KJV: "And we know that all things work together for good to them that love God, to them who are the called according to his purpose." I love this scripture because it doesn't say *some* things work together for the good but all things. No matter how bad it seems, how dark it looks, all things. That's why it's imperative to keep pushing. Don't give up; don't give in. We serve a God of a second chance. He is going to keep working until it becomes good in your life.

You must continue in your process no matter how it feels or what it looks like because it grows you up. And here is a kingdom secret that will help you endure the test of time as God is purifying you. As you're executing your kingdom mandate, learn to serve God without conditions. Whether it's a good day, a bad day, a sunny day or a rainy day, you continue in God. Why? It grows you up, it matures you for the next level you're getting ready to walk into.

God is raising end time vessels to win end time battles. To undo heavy burdens and lead the body into total and complete deliverance. So whatever you do, don't stop pushing. Every time I look back at what God did and how He is moving, it blows my mind. I am just in awe of God and His goodness. For me, looking back five years this is the promise God gave me. Which brings me to this scripture: "Then said the Lord unto me, Thou hast well seen: for I will hasten my word to perform it."

This next move of God is not a usual move and God is looking for vessels He can use in this hour. We are entering into the days of revival fire; that's why it's important to go through your process. Let God be God in your life. Let Him shift your prayer life, how you move and go about things. Let God orchestrate it all for His glory. It's imperative not to let any offenses arise or remain in your heart. Your walk with God is capped off in the place of offense. We must remember the thing we struggle in with in life is the part of us not surrendered to God. Division halts the move of God. Heart issues hinder the flow of God. Don't allow anything to remain that displeases God. Humility will take you where pride can't. I had to realize this myself and I promise you when I truly started walking in love, I attracted the right relationships. Mighty things started transpiring in my life. I don't care to be right or wrong anymore, I just want to please God. This meant not just saying sorry but turning away from the thing that caused offense.

The last thing I want to share with you as you walk out your purpose and dream is allow God to bring about the right connections in your life. Don't rush God because you desire or want something badly. And please note if He speaks a thing, then that settles it. He will never be the author of confusion. There were some divine blessings I talked myself out of because of fear, but God graced me to regain them.

When I look back over my life, every season prepared me for the next. Everything happened to bring me right where I am today. Every dream and promise thus far that God declared over my life has manifested. The last storm taught me another level of warfare, I experienced God in way I never had. So every test and storm worked together for my good.

Here is one last powerful thing that God did in this season of my life. Let this be encouragement for you to keep pushing until you birth your God-given dream.

When I fell ill in 2013 from Guillain Barre Syndrome, I developed severe allergies. My lungs also were not 100 percent, which is why I was intubated a lot. I had to carry a EpiPen everywhere I went. Sometimes when I traveled, I would end up in ICU. Each of the allergies I had landed me in ICU fighting for my life on a ventilator. I was allergic to cinnamon as well, it was lethal. When God revealed to me my problem of fear and I yielded and got delivered, it shifted my entire life. Before this I was just hanging on to the promise that I would be completely healed one day.

The first miracle was God completely healing my lungs. Usually I would take medication and come close to being intubated and after the 58th time of being intubated I stayed in ICU. When God moved on me when I lost my baby, He began to restore everything. Because of my obedience He moved mightily.

I went to my lung appointment only to find out that for the first time since getting sick back in 2013 God had completely healed my lungs. When the nurse did my test and looked at my medical history and record, she was astounded. She checked my record a couple times. The doctor came in, looked at me and looked at the medical records. At that moment I knew God did it. The doctor said, "I don't know, but your lungs are completely healthy." He said, "The functionality of your lungs is that of a normal person." I asked for the report and I just blessed God. He is a promise keeper.

God was not finished with me yet, He was completing this thing in me. So I went out of town to a service at my leader's church. It was a deliverance service. The movement of God was thick up in there. I received a prayer for my womb only to go to the doctor the next day and find out through tests that God had wiped out every allergy I had. Once again God did it for me. I had anaphylactic allergies to so many medications and cinnamon. It was all untraceable in my body. Here is the crazy thing about it; it didn't hit me until I was home and ate cinnamon. Cinnamon used to close my airway. But I ate lot of it that day and nothing happened. We praised God that night in my house and cried. God did a whole miracle in my life. He took me from my death bed and raised me up all for His glory. He didn't stop there, He allowed me to go through a storm that altered my entire life. He then shifted me just to complete the promise in my life that I would be made whole.

I have never operated in this realm before in ministry like right now. This is why you can't give in; you can't throw in the towel. You have to keep pushing, keep pressing. Let God make His name great in you. I am so grateful for everything I have ever gone through and what God is doing right now. Be encouraged and know better is the ending of a thing than the beginning. It's not how you start but how you finish—finish strong!

Remember God is raising up voices that carry the fire of God in them. There is no compromise here, no mixture, carrying the full backing of heaven. It's time to execute the kingdom the way the Word of God declares. God is still moving in miracles, signs and wonders. He is a supernatural God moving in a supernatural way. There are no limits to what God can execute through us when we are one with Him.

I encourage you to be strong in the Lord and in the power of His might. Go deeper!

Ronisha's Acknowledgments

I truly bless the name of Jesus for everything He is doing in my life and the lives of His people. I know it's only because of God's grace that I am alive today. I want to thank my husband for being so amazing to me and always having my back. To my kids who most definitely keep me going. I thank God for Dr. Kishma for giving me this opportunity. I also give an honor to God for this divine season in my life and connecting me to greatness. I thank Him for my leaders who have poured tremendously into my life and my family; they truly are pillars in the body of Christ.

Meet author Ronisha Williams

My name is Prophetess Ronisha Williams; I am a servant, wife and mother. I am the founder and CEO of The Weight of Glory Ministries and author of four books, my last one being a bestseller, Beyond the Realm of You, God. I am an entrepreneur and radio show host of Matters of the Heart. I am a walking miracle, one who overcame death and being paralyzed losing my ability to do everything. I am a voice to the wounded and hope for the hopeless. God has truly given me a second chance and I owe my life to Him daily. This scripture sums it up. "I am crucified with Christ: nevertheless I live; yet not I, but Christ liveth in me: and the life which I now live in the flesh I live by the faith of the Son of God, who loved me, and gave himself for me." Galatians 2:20 KJV

Through God I have overcome so much in life. Philippians 1:6 is one of my favorite scriptures, I am confident in the very work God has begun in me. Everything I've gone through truly birthed the weight of God's glory in my life. I am seeing miracles

175

as God moves and shift things frequently.

No matter what you are facing in life, never measure your dreams, your destiny and purpose based off your circumstances. Every test and storm of life has an expiration date, keep pushing because greater awaits you. Remember the pressures of life can make you pitiful or powerful. Let them make you powerful as you execute your dreams and walk out destiny with purpose.

To learn more about me please visit www.ronishawilliams. com. I am also on Instagram @theglorycarrier, Facebook: Ronisha Williams.

Execute Your Dreams

By Kishma A. George

Several years ago, after I disconnected myself from the dream killers and began working on the vision, I remember sitting in the chair in my living room and the Lord gave me an assignment to host a fundraiser event for the non-profit organization. I was very excited about the project. I informed the board members and other people about the project. We started to plan four months ahead of the event. Everything was going well; the vendors registered, we got the funds for the location of the event, and the fliers to advertise the event were ready to be distributed. Everything you can think of was done to ensure a successful event. The day of the event came and I was very excited because, in my mind, the team had done a GREAT job marketing the event and HUNDREDS of people would show up...

The event started at 9:00 a.m. and by the time it turned 2:00 p.m. only 30 people had shown up at a facility that can hold over 500 people. After the event, I went home so disappointed with tears in my eyes. I felt as if I never wanted to come out of my bed again and face the board members or the world. The event in my eyes was truly a flop and not successful. I felt like a BIG failure. I told myself I would never host another event again for the rest of my life.

One day, during prayer, I was crying out to God asking why the event was not successful and what I did wrong. The Lord laid in my heart the thought that the event was a success because I completed the project. He reminded me that numbers did not matter; it is how the event was laid out in excellence. The Lord also reminded me to DREAM Again! Just because it did not work out the way I thought it should go did not mean it was not successful. God was teaching me to become successful; you have to learn from your failures what to do and what not to do. Moreover, the more you do anything the better you become as you go along. God was teaching me that He is guiding me, leading me, and encouraging me not to give up and to Dream Big!

The following year, the Lord laid in my heart to host another fundraiser event. I began this time by first seeking the face of God for instructions and directions. I made many changes to things I did at the last event. I worked harder and marketed the event a different way than I did it at the first event. At this second event, we had over 200 people, there were more vendors, and more tickets sold. The event was TRULY a BIG success!

So, I want to encourage you today that when you have a dream, do not give up. Even if you lose money pursuing your dreams, have people walking out on you, no one wants to fund your dreams, there's a lack of support, etc., DREAM Again AND DREAM BIG! Some of you reading this book, God showed you a vision that you will open a business, publish a book, write songs, teach, preach, open a shelter, write stage plays, open a non-profit, perhaps start a make-up line, open a clothing store, shoe store, a mini mall, be a mentor, produce music, write poetry, etc. and you ask God, "Can it really happen?"

God is saying, "Yes … if you only Believe!" God wants to bring forth the Dreamer in YOU! Remember, with God all things are POSSIBLE! God wants us to dream outside of the box.

Eph.3:20 states, "Now unto us who is able to do exceeding abundantly above all that we ask or think; according to the power that worketh in us." God's Word plainly and clearly stated our purpose, which is to be God's hands on this earth. He wants you to succeed, and if you are willing to step up to the plate, you will not fail because God will never leave you nor forsake you.

To every dreamer reading this, I want to encourage you to DREAM AGAIN! When you have a dream, walk by faith and not by sight. The belief that dreams are impossible to achieve stops people from getting what they really want. People are what they believe themselves to be. Proverbs 23:7 says, "For as he thinketh in his heart, so is he!" If you want success, start thinking of yourself as a success. True success is the progressive achievement of your God-inspired goals. Success is the result of living in alignment with God's laws of success.

God did not make you with limitations… Mark 9:23 says, "All things are possible to him that believeth." Believe that new and exciting opportunities are coming your way in this NEW SEASON because God is not through blessing you! Whatever vision He has shown you, believe His Word and step out in faith until it is manifested in your life.

Kingdom Wealth!

Psalm 1:3 - And he shall be like a tree planted by the rivers of water, that bringeth forth his fruit in his season; his leaf also shall not wither; and whatsoever he doeth shall prosper.

5 STEPS TO TURN YOUR DREAM INTO A PROFITBALE BUSINESS

1. Write down all the dreams you would like to achieve this year.

_____

_____

_____

_____

_____

_____

_____

_____

_____

_____

_____

_____

_____

_____

_____

_____

2. Use what's in your hand.

Create a Signature Package Program or Six-Week Course and charge $997.00 (20 people) Total: $19,940.00

+++

Get 10 people weekly (for five days) to buy $2500.00 workshops, mentorship programs. - $25,000 weekly X 4 weeks = $100,000.00

+++

Get 50 people to register for your BOOT Camp and charge $1500 each for a Six-Week Program. Total: $75,000

+++

It's truly your time and SEASON to UNRAVEL what's in your HAND!

TOTAL: $194,940

3. Write down the scriptures to meditate on while pursuing your DREAMS.

_____

_____

_____

_____

_____

_____

_____

_____

_____

_____

4. Write down seven steps you will take to pursue your dreams.

_____

_____

_____

_____

_____

_____

_____

_____

_____

_____

5. Create a vision board of pictures of your dreams this year.

_____

_____

_____

_____

_____

_____

_____

_____

_____

_____

Kishma's Acknowledgements

First and foremost, I want to give God all the glory and honor, as He made this vision possible. I love You, Lord, with all my heart! ♡ In memory of my beloved father, Edmond Felix George; I am thankful for his encouragement and inspiring me to dream. ♡ To the best mother in the world, Novita Scatliffe-George; I thank you for your love, support, encouraging words and praying for me. Thank you for not giving up on me. I love you, Mom! ♡ To my wonderful daughter Kiniquá, I love you dearly. Thank you for your encouraging words, hugs and love. ♡ To my family; James, Raeisha, Christopher, Joshua, Seriah, Janisha and Kayla —thank you for supporting the vision with your prayers and love. ♡ Thank you Toy James and Abena Mc Clean, for your prayers, support and encouraging me to pursue my dreams. I thank God that you are my special friends. Love you, ladies. ♡

A special thank you to the co-authors of Birthing the Dreamer in You; Wanda Briscoe, Prophetess Nicole Bryant, Prophetess Shirlene Jones, Prophetess Rhaseeda Hague, Prophetess Ronisha Williams, Prophetess Ayanna Lynnay, Dominisha Senegal, Prophetess Chuntae Nicole, Pastor Rodney Davis, Dale Broome, Delsue Frankson, and Prophet Julian Jones.

A special thank you my beautiful Jackie Hicks for her amazing photography, beautiful Letitia Thornhill for her gift of makeup artistry, and beautiful Sonja Alston for an amazing hairstyle! Love you, ladies! ♡

To K.I.S.H. Home, Inc.'s board/advisors, volunteers and mentors; thank you for your dedication, support and believing in the vision of helping make a difference in the lives of young women in Delaware. To Emily Ann Warren, thank you for your support, love, and believing in me. To Pastor Ayanna, publisher; I thank God every day for bringing you into my life. You have been a blessing. Thank you for your encouraging words, support, love and believing in the vision. Love you♡ Lastly, but not least, I would like to thank CTS Graphics, ChosenButterfly Publishing and everyone who encouraged, prayed for and supported K.I.S.H. Home, Inc. over the years, I am forever grateful. God Bless!

Meet author Dr. Kishma A. George

Dr. Kishma can in a single phrase, be described as a Purpose Pusher. She is a prophetess, entrepreneur, inspirational speaker, international radio personality, TV show host, mentor, playwright, producer and 6x best-selling author, and her overarching mission is to inspire people to fulfill their God-given purpose. She believes that despite life's circumstances, there is greatness inside of you! Dr. Kishma's work as a speaker and mentor is executed through the Women Destined for Greatness Mentoring Program in Kent County, Delaware.

Dr. Kishma A. George is the president and CEO of K.I.S.H. (Kingdom Investments in Single Hearts) Home, Inc. K.I.S.H. Home, Inc. was founded out of the desire to make an impact in the lives of girls and women in Delaware, as well as those young women who are presently in or have aged out of the foster care system. Working as an independent living mentor Dr. George witnessed the tremendous challenges that aged out foster care youth experienced while trying to find their way to a self-sufficient and stable life.

A passion within her grew for these young adults and their future as she experienced their frustration in handling basic skills, such as opening a checking/savings account, parenting and the frustration of single parenthood. Ms. George knew that these young adults, whether they were a single parent or single, needed a strong support system that would empower and encourage them to take control of their lives. They struggled in their transition of leaving their homes or foster care because many were still attending high school and were not emotionally or financially stable.

After witnessing this, Ms. George began her journey of seeking ways to assist young adults in becoming emotionally and economically self-sufficient so that their transition out of their homes or the foster care system and into independent living would be successful. Many of the young adults with whom she worked left their homes or foster care at 18 years old and found themselves homeless, pregnant, lacking self-esteem, incarcerated, unemployed and without guidance. As a mentor, Ms. George became frustrated by the minimum amount of resources the community offered these young adults. She wanted to make a difference in their lives and make certain that they had a safe, successful transition to adulthood and independent living.

K.I.S.H. Home, Inc. offers young women in Delaware the support they need to become emotionally stable and self-sufficient in every aspect of their lives and community.

Her diligence and passion for young women have been recognized in various newspaper articles, including the *Dover Post*, *Delaware News Journal*, *Delaware State News*, and *Milford Beacon*. She was also featured in the *Kingdom Voices Magazine*, *Gospel 4 U Magazine*, *K.I.S.H. Magazine*, *BOND* Inc., and BlogSpot's week spotlight "Fostered Out of Love". In addition, she has appeared as a special guest on the *Atlanta LIVE* TV Show, *Life Talk* radio show with Coach TMB, the live TV Show *Straight Talk for Women Only*, and The *Frank and Travis Radio Show* on Praise 105.1.

Empowered Women Ministries have recognized Dr. Kishma as Woman of the Year in the category of entrepreneurial services, as well as Zeta Phi Beta Sorority, Inc. / Theta Zeta Zeta Chapter for her outstanding involvement in the Greater Dover Community. She was also presented with the Diversity Award (2013) from the State of Delaware / Social Services, the Authentic Servant Leadership Award (2014) & New Castle County Chapter of the DSU Alumni Association 33rd annual Scholarship Luncheon for outstanding service to the Wilmington Community and the Delaware State University (2014), Church Girlz Rock(2015); Humanitarian Award (2015), Faith Fighter Award (2016) , Business Woman of the Year (2106), CHOICES "Woman of the Year" (2016) and Global Smashers Award (2017). She has been awarded the Business Woman of the Year Award (2018), I AM Baby Doll Global Award (2018), I AM Entrepreneurship Devorah Award (2018), I AM Fabulous Award (2019), Phenomenal Woman of the Year (2019), and World-Changer Award (2019). Dr. Kishma received her Bachelor of Science degree in Psychology from Delaware State University and an Honorary Doctor of Philosophy; Humane Letters from CICA International University and Seminary. Her passion is to empower you through the Word of God and inspire you to begin living your DREAMS. No matter what your circumstances may be, God has a purpose for your life.

Dr. Kishma strives to make a difference in your life and make certain that YOU will birth EVERY DREAM God has placed on the inside. Dr. Kishma A. George is the director of the Women Destined for Greatness Mentoring Program and visionary/editor-in-chief for *K.I.S.H. Magazine*.

To Contact Kishma A. George visit www.kishmageorge.com.

Made in the USA
Monee, IL
24 September 2021

78165028R00108